HANDCRAFTED BITTERS

HANDCRAFTED

BITTERS

SIMPLE RECIPES for ARTISANAL BITTERS and the COCKTAILS that LOVE THEM

WILL BUDIAMAN

ROCKRIDGE PRESS

HOMEMADE BITTERS 101

New to the art of making your own bitters? These quick steps will have you mixing up your own bitters in no time:

1. **PICK YOUR METHOD.** There are two methods to making bitters: combine and infuse, and tincture. Before you get started, it's worth reading up on them a bit. See "The Method" in chapter 2 (page 40). The first four bitters recipes in each chapter use the combine and infuse method, and the last three use the tincture method.

2. **PICK A SEASON.** The recipe chapters in this book are divided by season, featuring the finest ingredients year-round.

3. **START MAKING SOME BITTERS!** If you're using the first method, just follow the directions outlined in the recipe. Your bitters will be ready in 3½ weeks. The steps for this method are identical every time—only the ingredients change. If you're using the second method, your mileage will vary—see page 45 to find out how long each tincture will take.

CONTENTS

FOREWORD

Many industries have a pivotal moment that innovates or changes it forever; for the electronics industry, it was moving from tubes to transistors; for the spirits industry, it was bitters. Before the introduction of bitters, spirits were harsh and often unapproachable. With the advent of bitters and tinctures, the modern-day cocktail was formed.

Most people think of Angostura when they hear the term bitters, but bitters are as varied and dynamic as spirits themselves. Leading up to prohibition, bitters were not only for cocktails, but were also used as remedies for a variety of ailments. Angostura itself often served as a remedy for seasickness. After prohibition, many of these bitters went the way of the dinosaur. But with the resurgence of the cocktail culture and craft bitters today, the market has filled with hundreds of new and diverse flavors. For the most part, cocktails consist of a spirit, a sweet or sour element, and the key ingredient: a bitter or tincture. Thanks to the concept of mixology, there is literally no limit to the flavor profile of a cocktail.

At Future Bars in San Francisco and the East Bay, we have focused on providing an array of customer-centric experiences which offer flavor profiles that cannot be experienced anywhere else. These complex flavors are accentuated and comprised of our twenty-odd bitters and fifty-plus tinctures, including such unique flavors as tobacco, mole, lapsang souchong, fo-ti, and many more. We have also been using barrel aging to add more complexity to our bitters. Our central commissary is headed by Sarah Shaw. "I'll put anything in a jar and cover it with Everclear, just to see what will happen," Sara said. "The tinctures I find most interesting are the unconventional ones, such as Candy Cap mushroom, cedarwood, and leather. With bitters, the biggest challenge is usually getting a high flavor concentration without distortion. Most bitters go through at least three or four versions until I get a flavor that I like and that will stand up in a cocktail. Some, like celery and peach, had to go through seven or eight incarnations before I was happy with them. With tinctures, the biggest challenge is consistency. We use natural ingredients, so there's always a level of variance in the botanical we begin with. Since the infusion time is shorter than it is for bitters, and because they are mostly single-note flavors, there's less room for error."

Many of the bitters and tinctures are a challenge to develop, but when they come out well, they are the key to creating an innovative cocktail.

Running multiple establishments that offer libations with complex flavor profiles has challenges, and many creations that will not translate well into home use. It is also important to keep costs of production down (perhaps by making larger volumes), thus keeping cocktails reasonably priced. While we primarily use our own bitters, we also use traditional bitters and craft-produced bitters as well. Fee Brothers, Scrappy's, Bitter truth, Bittermen's, and Angostura are some examples of these. In my opinion, The Bitter End in Santa Fe has created a very innovative line of bitters with flavors like Jamaican Jerk and Memphis Barbecue.

I get a great deal of pleasure in sharing a cocktail I have made with my own ingredients, whether a distilled spirit, aged cocktail, infused spirit, or bitters and tinctures. With simple ingredients, a high-proof base like Everclear, and the recipes in this book as your guide, you can get started on your way to crafting a cocktail with ingredients you love.

Much like being a chef—and bitters can also be used in culinary art—you should never be afraid to experiment or fail, because you can always use perceived failures as a starting point toward creating something truly unique and wonderful.

—Doug Dalton

INTRODUCTION

**"You need three ingredients for a cocktail.
Vodka and Mountain Dew is an emergency."**

PEGGY OLSON, *MAD MEN*

The classic line from Peggy Olson, Don Draper's ambitious young protégée in the television show *Mad Men*, best sums up a cocktail: an alcohol (vodka), some flavoring (Mountain Dew), and that unmentioned third ingredient. That would be bitters. These days the term *cocktail* is used to refer to any drink containing liquor, but originally bitters were an integral part of the very definition of a cocktail.

In today's hot landscape of celebrity mixologists and craft cocktails, you've likely used bitters when making yourself a cocktail at home or noticed them at your local establishment. But do you really understand the magic of bitters?

Bitters are a flavoring agent prepared using botanical material (such as roots, barks, flowers, or fruits) mixed with alcohol and a little water. Bitters unite flavors that otherwise might not work well together in a cocktail. Take a classic cocktail, such as the Old Fashioned. Ask a bartender to make one with bitters and one without, and the difference will be like night and day. Chances are the one without bitters won't taste very good. The one with them, if made correctly, will be delicious, all because the bitters are marrying the flavors—

in this case, sweet vermouth, sugar, and rye. When all is said and done, bitters are an ingredient a good cocktail cannot do without.

There are many bitters available on the market, from the classics such as Angostura, to some with witty names such as Issan Another Level (a reference to the cooking of a region in northeastern Thailand), to others with innovative flavors such as chocolate mole. But serious bars serving serious cocktails have taken the extra step of making their own, setting themselves apart from drink slingers. Here's the secret, though: Bitters are not that difficult to make, so there's no reason why you shouldn't be able to up your cocktail-mixing skills. If you're ready to make your own bitters and mix up some serious cocktails, then this is the book for you.

Part 1 covers what you need to get started, with an overview of bitters' history—from their origins as medicine, to their near disappearance after Prohibition, to their resurgence with today's craft cocktail movement. You'll also find out about the two main techniques used to create bitters, plus the necessary equipment and ingredients. Part 2 features a plethora of bitters recipes. Each bitters recipe is followed by two cocktail recipes, so that you get a sense of how flavor pairings work. The chapters are organized by season, and the bitters recipes in each chapter will allow you to practice the two bitters-making techniques.

With excellent recipes and sound advice, you'll be well on your way to impressing your friends with your newfound bartending skills. So what are you waiting for? Start polishing your glasses.

Behind the Bar

TOBIN LUDWIG, CO-FOUNDER, HELLA BITTERS

Making bitters takes time and patience. Failure is an important part of the process. You often can't predict the way the ingredients will infuse. There's also no perfect science to how much of each ingredient to use. Some spices and bittering agents are very volatile, and others are much milder. Always keep a pen and paper close by and take meticulous notes as you experiment.

When we made our first big batch of our citrus bitters—which included black peppercorns as one of its aromatics—we tasted it a few days in, and it was immensely peppery. Normally the peppercorns stay in the formula the full thirty days. Luckily we keep all of our spices in mesh bags, so I could fish out the peppercorns and hope the other ingredients would balance out because the batch was too big to abandon. With some luck, at the end of the month the bitters ended up being wonderful, with the black pepper being nothing more than a subtle addition to citrusy goodness.

The biggest challenge we've faced when making small batch bitters is consistency. We use whole spices, cut and sifted bitter agents, and fresh fruit. The intensity of these ingredients varies seasonally so using the same weight and identical formula doesn't guarantee an identical result.

Choosing our favorite bitters is like asking us to choose between our children, but we're really into our Smoked Chili. We love that these bitters impart both spice (heat) and smoke into a recipe.

Hella Bitters are all natural, made in small batches, and offer a premium alternative to all that mass-produced stuff out there. Founded in Brooklyn and thriving in NYC, Hella Bitters' passion for quality has been there since the beginning and it's how they went from being a weekend project, to a bitters company in serious pursuit of the delicious.

PART ONE

GETTING STARTED

CHAPTER ONE

A BITTERS RENAISSANCE

Cocktails have come a long way in the past decade, and it's a very exciting time to be a professional or amateur bartender. At any bar intent on making top-quality mixed drinks, you'll find that mixologists have cast an eye to the heyday of cocktails for inspiration, using fresh fruit juices, high-quality spirits, and bespoke bitters as the order of the day. And looking back has inspired more than just the revival of delicious drinks: Speakeasy-style bars, with a hidden entrance, low lighting, and impeccably dressed bartenders, now seem almost ubiquitous; and whether you love them or find them pretentious, it's hard to ignore the role they've played in helping generate an awareness of old-school cocktails. Bitters, in particular, have sparked yet another do-it-yourself movement among food and drink connoisseurs.

OFFICIALLY EMBITTERED

It's hard to believe that bitters fell off the drinks map for a long time, but they did. Now, thanks to a renewed interest in classic cocktails, bitters are alive and well. But what do they really mean for your cocktails, and how did they become so popular?

THE COMEBACK KID

Just a little more than a decade ago, the odds were stacked against any sort of bitters revival. In fact, in 2004, there were just three brands of aromatic bitters available on the market: Angostura, Peychaud's, and Fee Brothers' orange bitters. Unless you were a bartender they were an obscure ingredient, and if you did tend bar, chances were hardly anyone ever asked about them.

Today there are hundreds and the list keeps growing every day. Moreover, bartenders at the country's best bars are expected to cater to increasingly savvy consumers with an array of bitters, either made by small-batch producers or made in-house.

>> Angostura bitters are named after the city in Venezuela where they were invented (the city was renamed Ciudad Bolivar in 1846), but the company is now headquartered in Trinidad. <<

What kick-started the renaissance? Chalk it up to an increased interest in classic cocktails, in which bitters play a key role, spurred on by the rise of food media and their entrance into pop culture. Television shows such as *Mad Men*, with its highly stylized view of 1960s-era cocktail culture, helped build momentum for the introduction of retro drinks—including the Old Fashioned, the Manhattan, and the Sidecar—to a new generation.

If, like many, you found yourself inspired by that show to find a nice bar and order an Old Fashioned for the first time, you probably asked the bartender what was in your drink. "Rye, vermouth, sugar, and bitters," came the reply, which might well have raised the question, What are bitters?

Bitters are a key ingredient in creating many classic and modern cocktails. Before delving into that discussion, though, it's a good idea to take a step back and talk a little bit about the two main types of bitters: potable bitters and aromatic bitters.

Potable bitters are liqueurs that have been sweetened and flavored with fresh or dried plant-based ingredients. They generally have a lower alcohol content than aromatic bitters and are drinkable all on their own. The liqueurs Jägermeister, Campari, and Fernet-Branca, served before or after meals to stimulate appetite or aid digestion, are examples of potable bitters. They are sometimes used as a cocktail ingredient but are measured by the jigger.

Aromatic bitters are the subject of this book. Like potable bitters, they are flavored with plant-based ingredients—anything from apples, allspice, or gentian root to orange zest, saffron, or wild cherry bark. They have an alcohol content of about 45 percent by volume and are meant to be added to a drink a few drops at a time. When bartenders today mention bitters, they're referring to aromatic bitters.

Aromatic bitters bring balance and harmony to cocktails. The idea of using something that tastes bitter to make your drinks taste better might seem counterintuitive. After all, when you're young, you automatically avoid foods that taste bitter because bitterness can signal poison. But the older you get, the better you understand how bitterness works in our edible world, and you learn that some of your favorite foods have a bitter element to them. Many fine olive oils, chocolates, and wines taste best when the right amount of bitterness is present.

Just as a burst of acidity will liven up a dish, a dash of bitters will mean the difference between a flat or overly sweet cocktail and a balanced one. Or, as Jennifer McLagan puts it in her cookbook *Bitter: A Taste of the World's Most Dangerous Flavor, with Recipes*, "In the kitchen, eschewing bitter is like cooking without salt, or eating without looking. Without bitterness we lose a way to balance sweetness, and by rejecting it we limit our range of flavors. Food without bitterness lacks depth and complexity." And the same is true for cocktails.

Old Fashioned

For many cocktail enthusiasts, an Old Fashioned is the go-to order upon arriving at an unfamiliar bar. But what separates a good Old Fashioned from a bad one?

Bitters—Angostura bitters, to be exact. Without them, the cocktail would taste sweet, and only sweet. Bitters bring balance and complexity to the mixture.

Like many classic cocktails, the Old Fashioned has evolved since it was first conceived. Although it's impossible to pin down an exact date, probably sometime in the 1880s, a bartender at the Pendennis Club in Louisville, Kentucky, started serving it. From there, it made its way to the original Waldorf-Astoria Hotel bar, thanks to Colonel James E. Pepper, a bourbon distiller.

The first published recipe appeared in Harry Johnson's *Bartenders' Manual*, the first edition of which appeared in 1882. Johnson called it an Old Fashioned Whiskey Cocktail, and it had Curaçao, the orange-flavored liqueur with the signature blue hue.

The closest predecessor to today's version, however, appeared in 1895 in *Modern American Drinks* by George J. Kappeler. His recipe called for sugar and water crushed together, Angostura, ice, lemon peel, and a measure of whiskey. Note that there was no orange or maraschino cherry involved.

It's not certain when those fruits replaced the lemon peel, but they have become the norm. Today some bartenders even go so far as to mash them together with the sugar cube and bitters. Others liken this to making sangria out of a classic, and deplore the practice. But one thing hasn't changed: the use of Angostura bitters.

A BRIEF HISTORY OF BITTERS

Antiquated forms of bitters have been found in many ancient sites. In fact, evidence shows that ancient Egyptians were using an early form of bitters (herbs mixed into wine) to treat illnesses; for the purposes of this book, the turn of the eighteenth century, when bitters as they are known today were in their embryonic stage, is a good place to start. Around that time, English physicians prescribed bitters as a cure for all manner of ailments—stomach, kidney, liver, blood ailments—you name it, there was a bitters tonic for it. The bitters at the time were potable, but just because they were quaffed by the mouthful does not mean they were palatable. Toward the end of the eighteenth century, the English in particular had taken to mixing bitters with fortified wines from the Canary Islands or combining them with brandy to improve the taste, and these bitters were sold as hangover cures, ironically. The next logical step to making these tonics more drinkable was adding sugar, and something resembling a cocktail was born, although the word itself wouldn't come into use until later.

The first mention of bitters as a cocktail ingredient appeared in 1806 in an article in *The Balance and Columbian Repository*, a Hudson, New York, newspaper. In this article, Harry Croswell explained that *"Cock-tail* is a stimulating liquor, composed of spirits of any kind, sugar, water, and bitters." But in the United States at that time, bitters were considered more medicine than drink mixer and were typically imbibed straight. They had become extremely popular, with hundreds of brands to choose from. Unsavory salesmen took advantage of the popularity of bitters, selling tonics purporting to cure anything, even blindness.

Two bitters from that time remain popular today and were created by actual medical practitioners: Angostura and Peychaud's bitters. Dr. Johann Siegert, surgeon general in Simon Bolivar's army in Venezuela, created Angostura aromatic bitters (initially named Amargo Aromatico) around 1820 in the town of Angostura. The tonic was used to treat digestive problems in soldiers. Antoine Peychaud, a Creole pharmacist in New Orleans, created his eponymous bitters in the late 1830s. Also prescribed for stomach ailments, Peychaud's bitters were often mixed into Cognac.

Bitters arrived as a true ingredient of the cocktail during the golden age of cocktails in the late nineteenth century, though they still straddled a line between recreational and medicinal use. That vibrant period birthed classics such as the Sazerac; sumptuous hotel bars, including the Waldorf-Astoria's, were the height of glamour; and the skills of bartenders were held in high regard. But the tide was changing still. At the dawn of the twentieth century, the government passed the Pure Food and Drug Act, imposing safety regulations on the bitters market. As a result, many of the fly-by-night manufacturers went out of business. This paved the way for the trustworthy brands to complete the transition from medicine to cocktail ingredient.

>> Just five people at the House of Angostura know the secret recipe for its famous bitters. <<

In 1920, just as the cocktail movement reached full swing, Prohibition went into effect. At that point, even legitimate bitters businesses began dying out. Peychaud's, Angostura, and a few smaller brands were all that were left. Peychaud's survived thanks to the unique illicit cocktail culture of New Orleans, and Angostura, which was not based in the United States, had an international clientele.

With few exceptions, classic cocktails and cocktail culture went on hiatus during Prohibition. The quality of liquors declined considerably during that time. Spirits sold on the black market were sometimes adulterated with dangerous compounds, and bartenders did what they could to make these substandard liquors taste acceptable, resorting to the heavy use of juices, syrups, and even ice cream. This trend continued even after Prohibition was repealed (one explanation for the popularity of flabby drinks such as Sex on the Beach,

Key Dates in Bitters History

1712. In England, Stoughton Bitters successfully patents its product.

1750. The practice of mixing bitters with brandy and sugar becomes commonplace in England; the mixture is used as a hangover cure and medicine.

1806. The earliest printed record in America of the meaning of the word *cocktail* appears in a newspaper, *The Balance and Columbian Repository*.

1824. In Venezuela, Dr. Johann Siegert completes his work on a bitters recipe aimed at relieving stomach ailments, dubbed Siegert's Amargo Aromatico, known today as Angostura aromatic bitters.

1838. In a shop located in the New Orleans French Quarter, Antoine Peychaud, a pharmacist from Haiti, starts offering his unique bitters with a splash of Cognac to customers.

1870. Dr. Siegert dies and the makers of Angostura move their operations from Venezuela to Trinidad.

1906. The Pure Food and Drug Act passes.

1920. Prohibition begins.

1933. Prohibition ends.

1951. Fee Brothers debuts its orange bitters, the first new bitters product to hit the market since the end of Prohibition, but purchasing the bitters proves to be an elusive proposition for all but the most determined connoisseurs.

piña colada, and frozen daiquiris during the 1970s). It was no surprise, then, that during Prohibition many of America's best bartenders moved to Europe and other parts of the world.

Dale DeGroff at the Rainbow Room in Manhattan is widely credited with helping spur the return to classic cocktails in the late 1980s. When devising the menu for the bar's opening, he looked to old cocktail books for inspiration. DeGroff's work has made him a role model for up-and-coming bartenders.

Around the same time, Gary and Mardee Regan began working on their very own orange bitters, spurred by a futile search for a commercially available one that began when they sought to recreate cocktails from pre-Prohibition days. In 2005 they at last perfected the formula for Regan's Orange Bitters No. 6, the first new bitters to become widely available since the 1950s.

>> Cognac with a splash of Peychaud's bitters was the precursor to the Sazerac, a classic cocktail from New Orleans. Imbibers sipped from cone-shaped cups called coquetiers—drink enough of them, and that delicious French word starts looking like one possible origin of the word "cocktail" (albeit, while other things become hazy). <<

Today, the bitters market is growing by leaps and bounds. There are hundreds if not thousands of choices that did not exist a decade ago, whether from large commercial producers or small artisanal operations.

Sazerac

Ask a local in New Orleans where to get the best Sazerac,
and they'll likely tell you about Hermes Bar at Antoine's, or the
Sazerac Bar at the Roosevelt. You can't go wrong with either.

But ask who invented it, and you'll get many answers.

Like the origin of many classic cocktails, the origin of the Sazerac
is probably best relegated to the genre of lore rather than history.
Its creation didn't happen at a single point in time; rather, it was
an evolution.

In 1838, Antoine Peychaud, a pharmacist from Haiti, started serving his unique bitters with a splash of Cognac at his shop in the
French Quarter. The mixture proved to be popular, and soon resi-
dents started asking for the drink in the coffeehouses of the area.
(*Coffeehouse* was actually a common euphemism for a place
serving liquor.) In 1850 the Sazerac Coffee House began making
the same drink, but with a brand of Cognac that bore the name
of the coffeehouse. A bartender there, Leon Lamothe, came up
with the addition of absinthe, and at last the formula was complete and the drink had a name: Sazerac.

There was one final change that occurred sometime in the 1870s,
and that was the switch from Cognac (or brandy) to rye. An
insect infestation had decimated the vineyards of France, making
wine, and consequently brandy, scarce.

After that change, the Sazerac continued to live on. What you
could never replace, though, are Peychaud's bitters, because
without them, a Sazerac simply isn't a Sazerac.

WHY MAKE YOUR OWN BITTERS?

There are plenty of reasons to make your own bitters. But the most important reason is one that you already knew when you picked up this book: Working on a kitchen project that takes time and patience gives you a sense of fulfillment that you can get only by making something from scratch.

See something you like at the farmers' market? Use it to make bitters. If it's summertime, perhaps a local variety of peach has caught your taste buds' attention with its notes of vanilla and cinnamon. Marry it with those two ingredients and use it in a cocktail, even one that doesn't normally call for bitters. That Bellini at Sunday brunch? It's practically demanding it.

Or perhaps it's fall and fruit stands are bursting with apples. Concoct your very own apple bitters, and be daring with them: Take a classic such as the Old Fashioned (page 70), and add a dash of fall with apple and clove bitters. Or just follow the recipe for the Fall Fashioned (page 167). You get the idea.

But the main reason is that it's nice to know exactly what's going into your bitters. You can choose to use organic fruits and nuts, fair trade chocolate and coffee, and nonirradiated spices if you wish; you can decide what type and brand of spirit to use as a base; and you can toast, crush, chop, and grind to your heart's content.

And let's not forget the mystique factor, because when you tell your friends exactly what's in their drink—horehound, orris root, quassia, and wormwood—they'll think you're a wizard.

Of course, there is one big pragmatic reason for making your own bitters. Commercially produced bitters are expensive: A 10-ounce bottle of Peychaud's costs about $15; a 16-ounce bottle of Angostura goes for about $30. And the stuff from smaller producers, which comes in interesting and esoteric flavors, including chocolate mole, kaffir lime, Buddha's hand (an exotic citrus fruit that looks like fingers), and sriracha, can be both pricey and hard to find.

Behind the Bar

MILES THOMAS, FOUNDER, SCRAPPY'S BITTERS

A good bitters should, when properly paired with your base spirit or mix, serve only to elevate the drink. For example, if you are using a young whiskey, which has a tendency to be a bit hot, the bitters should make it smooth and round. If you are using an older spirit that is already smooth, they can bring out some of the more unique or subtle notes to the front of the palate that may have otherwise gone unnoticed. In addition, they can add complexity to a sometimes one-dimensional spirit. The different bitters flavors each have their own respective characteristics that can take the spirit or mix in different directions; the key is to pair these flavors properly.

Oftentimes, the bitters become the link that brings all the flavors of a cocktail together, a sort of bonding flavor in a mixture that would have otherwise seemed disjointed. The degree of success in any of these instances is directly proportional to the quality of ingredients used to make the bitters and the method of extraction, of which there are many. The key is to find the right method for the right ingredients.

Seattle bartender Miles Thomas founded Scrappy's Bitters in 2008. By selecting the finest ingredients possible and holding every batch to the same impeccable standards, Scrappy's delivers a bolder, truer flavor, making the best bitters for the best bartenders.

CHAPTER TWO

THE BITTERS LAB

Now that the history lesson is over, it's time to put together your shopping list for ingredients, tools, and equipment; get some money-saving tips; and learn about the two main techniques for making bitters. By the time you finish, you'll be well prepared to tackle the recipes in part 2.

THE INGREDIENTS

There are three groups of ingredients that go into making bitters: bittering agents, flavoring agents, and spirits. Although some of the ingredients might sound exotic, there's no need to worry because this section will guide you every step of the way.

BITTERING AGENTS

Bittering agents are the foundation for your witch's brew. Without them, you couldn't call your creations bitters. Although they have mysterious-sounding names—your bitters ingredient list could read like something that would make Professor Severus Snape of the Hogwarts School of Witchcraft and Wizardry proud—rest assured that the ones listed here can be found without too much work, that they come from a plant grown on planet Earth, and that, in fact, many of them are used to make therapeutic teas.

>> In 2009, the makers of Angostura, a key ingredient in Old Fashioned cocktails and Manhattans, struggled to keep up with demand for their product, leading to a shortage that lasted until April 2010. Bartenders across the country undertook fevered searches for a replacement—a tall order. <<

Here are some of the most common agents, listed in order of increasing bitterness.

- WILD CHERRY BARK. This dried bark has a pronounced aroma that is sweet and fruity, with notes of cinnamon. Flavors of cherry and vanilla soothe the palate. Some good pairings include almonds, chocolate, and other dark stone fruit.

- ORRIS ROOT. The root of the Florentine iris has a sweet, floral, and slightly nutty aroma that is reminiscent of talcum. Its flavor is delicate and woody; pairings include apples and pears.

- HOREHOUND. This dried herb has well-balanced flavor and aroma and is a good all-purpose bittering agent.

- CINCHONA BARK. This dried bark is the source of quinine in tonic water, a treatment for malaria. It leaves strong floral notes on the palate, and the aroma is warm and sweet with lemon peel notes. It would be equally at home in citrus bitters paired with gin drinks or in spiced bitters, such as cinnamon, allspice, or nutmeg.

- GENTIAN ROOT. The first impression is that of spring, both in aroma and flavor. It reminds you of all the beautiful green things on display at the farmers' market. (Or, oddly enough, raw bean sprouts, if you've had experience with them.) This dried root would pair well with anything leafy and herbaceous.

- WORMWOOD. Anyone who has sampled absinthe will be surprised to discover that wormwood doesn't smell or taste like licorice (that component of absinthe actually derives from anise). Instead, it smells like lemongrass without the tang. Its bitterness dominates all and can only be compared to eating a large chunk of grapefruit pith, meaning it will stand up to bold flavors. But it does turn liquids green.

FLAVORING AGENTS

Many of these ingredients are probably already in your kitchen. Flavoring agents are whatever ingredients you'd like your bitters to taste like. The following list outlines broad categories but is not meant to be exhaustive.

- CHOCOLATE. Cacao nibs yield incomparable flavor, and chocolate bitters are a nice complement to a bold, Scotch-based drink.

- COFFEE BEANS. Try experimenting with single-origin beans from different parts of the world or different roasts to give your bitters a signature flavor.

- DRIED CHILES. Chipotle, ancho, and guajillo are good ones to start with; they can add smoky or savory complexity to tequila- and mezcal-based drinks. But there are tons of other chiles to choose from.

- FRUIT PEELS. Take inspiration from the farmers' market, and use whatever looks fresh. Buy organic when possible.

- HERBS. The sky's the limit—basil, cilantro, mint, parsley, rosemary, sage, thyme. As long as it's fresh, give it a shot.

- NUTS. Almonds, pistachios, hazelnuts, walnuts, or any other nut you can think of—be sure to try them all!

- SPICES. Spices present many possibilities, which can seem overwhelming at first. One way to think about them is in terms of seasons. Some examples: spicy cinnamon for fall apples, licorice-scented fennel seeds for winter citrus, and lime-flavored coriander for tropical summer drinks.

SPIRITS

The last thing to consider is what kind of spirit you're going to use. When alcohol comes into contact with an agent, it pulls out the essential oils, which carry flavors and aromas. So the more alcohol a spirit has, the sooner your bitters will be ready.

Look for neutral spirits such as Everclear grain alcohol or vodka that is at least 45 percent alcohol by volume. Purchase the highest-quality spirits you can afford—your ingredients may end up soaking in it for up to a month.

Bourbon, rye, tequila, and rum can also be used if they match up with the flavors you're using.

Sourcing Ingredients

Sourcing ingredients for your bitters project might seem like a challenge, but with a little research you should be able to find everything you need.

For dried herbs and spices, look to local spice shops. Many stores, including Patel Brothers (www .patelbros.com) and Kalustyan's (www.kalustyans.com), ship nation-wide, and some spice shops also carry a selection of bittering agents.

Restaurant supply stores are a great place to pick up spices in bulk: Because they cater to food service operations, spices are sold in one-pound (or larger) containers and are much cheaper than what you would pay at a supermarket.

Holistic apothecaries, such as the Dandelion Botanical Company (www.dandelionbotanical.com) and Tenzing Momo (www.tenzingmomo .com), are also a good source of dried herbs and are your best bet for sourcing bittering agents.

Finding the best-quality ingredients should be your top priority when making bitters. That said, it's help-ful to keep a few money-saving tips in mind.

START SMALL. If you're new to making bitters, start by purchasing small amounts of ingredients, and purchase only the ones you need. Dried herbs and spices have a shelf life and lose potency over time.

BUY IN BULK. If you know you're going to use a particular ingredient frequently, it pays to buy in bulk. If you have access to a warehouse shopping club, you can also save substantially on spirits, which will be your largest expense.

AVOID GROUND INGREDIENTS. Although ground roots, barks, and spices may shorten the amount of time required to make bitters, they are difficult to strain out. They also have a shorter shelf life.

AVOID THE TUMBLEWEEDS. Shop at a store that is well trafficked; high turnover means fresher ingredients.

LAST CALL. If you visit a farmers' market near closing time, you might be able to score some top-notch produce at a discount.

THE SUPPLIES

Just as important as the ingredients are the tools of the trade.

NEED-TO-HAVE

Here are the tools you need to get started making your own bitters at home, as well as some great cocktails. Some of these items are probably in your kitchen already.

- BAR SPOON. You'll want a metal spoon with a long handle that is twisted in the middle to make stirred drinks in a mixing glass.

- BAR TOWELS. Look for ribbed terry towels made from 100 percent high-grade absorbent cotton for maximum durability and effectiveness.

- CHEESECLOTH. A finely woven food-safe cloth is essential for making bitters. Use it to strain flavoring and bittering agents out of the spirits. Look for cheesecloth that is 100 percent cotton; unbleached and reusable cheesecloth is also available.

- CORKSCREW. There are many types to choose from, including the winged corkscrew, waiter's corkscrew, and the Rabbit; select the one you're most comfortable using. The winged corkscrew is easy to use, the waiter's corkscrew is compact, and the Rabbit looks good and is easy to use, but it's also pricey.

- CUTTING BOARD. A wooden cutting board with rubber feet is a solid choice: It's easy on your knives, preserving their edges longer, and has a nonslip grip on the work surface.

- FUNNELS. Funnels make it easy to pour liquids into containers without spilling. You'll need a small one for transferring liquids into small glass bottles (make sure the stem will fit) and a large one to use with glass jars (make sure the mouth diameter is large enough that the funnel can rest on the lip).

Behind the Bar

ELANA LEPOWSKI, CREATOR OF STIRANDSTRAIN.COM

The best piece of advice I can give someone starting out with bitters is to mark your calendar! While your bitters are brewing away in a cool, dark place, it's easy to forget that they exist. I've found that setting up reminders on my phone's calendar for when to strain, when to let sit, when to bottle, helped a lot in making sure I didn't lose my hard work. There's nothing worse than zesting thirty lemons for bitters only to see the whole lot end up in the garbage.

Speaking of lemons, my favorite bitters to make are my Meyer Lemon Bitters. My mother-in-law has a large Meyer lemon tree at her house that always produces more lemons than we need. I use those Meyer lemons mixed in with some Eureka lemons, Kaffir lime leaves, coriander and any other random citrus that I'm overstocked with. It has a great combination of sweet and spice, and the best part is that every season it's slightly different based on what is available, a lot like a vintage of wine. So I make a point to batch it every year.

One misconception people have about making bitters at home is that you need to large batch all the time, because so many recipes out there seem to yield servings for a crowd. Not true! You can always scale bitters back, especially if it's a batch just for your own home, or for bottling and giving away during the holidays.

The Stir and Strain blog is a go-to creative resource for cocktail enthusiasts. The blog features original cocktail recipes as well as variations on classics, plus a weekly round up of Booze News from around the web. Mixing cocktails out of her home bar, host Elana Lepkowski develops drinks for everyone from the cocktail novice to the behind-the-bar professional.

- GLASS BOTTLES. Look for 2- to 5-ounce glass bottles with tight seals. Clear bottles are useful for making small amounts of tinctures, allowing you to see the color changes. Dark bottles with a built-in dropper are useful for storing finished bitters or tinctures for later use.

- GLASS JARS. Pint- or quart-size clear jars with tight-fitting lids are useful for making bitters using the "combine and infuse" method and also for making large batches of tinctures.

- HAWTHORNE STRAINER. This strainer is for making cocktails designed to be used with the metal cup of a Boston shaker or a mixing glass. The design features a coiled wire, which goes inside the perimeter, and four dimples, which help hold the strainer in place as you pour.

- ICE TONGS AND BUCKET. If you're planning on making several cocktails, it's nice to be prepared. Placing all your ice in a bucket in advance and using tongs will make "service" flow more smoothly.

- ICE TRAYS. For making cocktails, look for two different types of ice trays: a plastic one that makes 1-inch cubes, which will be used for chilling shaken drinks, and a silicone one that makes 2-inch cubes, for drinks that are served on the rocks.

- JIGGER. This metal measuring cup is used for making cocktails. The design features two cones joined together, and each side has a different measurement. The usual pairing is 1 and 1½ ounces, but other sizes are also available.

- KNIVES. A sharp paring knife is essential for working with smaller fruit, such as limes or oranges, while a chef's knife is needed for larger fruit such as grapefruit. A serrated bread slicer is effective on pineapples and tomatoes.

- LABELS. Look for small address labels at your office supply store; they're the perfect size and adhere well to glass, so you can keep all your bitters straight.

- MIXING GLASS. A mixing glass is ideal for making stirred drinks using a bar spoon. If you have a Boston shaker, you already have one; otherwise, you can purchase one separately. They look like beer pint glasses.

- MUDDLER. This wooden implement has one flat end and one rounded end. The flat side is used to crush sugar cubes, fruit, herbs, and spices at the bottom of a mixing glass.

- PEELERS. You'll need one to peel zest from fruit. A side vegetable peeler is easiest to use for beginners; Swiss peelers create wider strips of zest.

- ROLLING PIN, MALLET, OR OTHER HEAVY OBJECT. Sometimes a cocktail recipe will call for crushed ice. If your freezer doesn't have a built-in ice maker, you can improvise. Place 1-inch cubes in a resealable bag and crush with a rolling pin, a mallet, or the back of a heavy pan.

- SHAKER. Two types predominate. A cocktail shaker has a strainer built into its domed top, which is nice, but a Boston shaker, which consists of a mixing glass and a larger metal cup, is more versatile, allowing you to make both shaken and stirred drinks.

NICE-TO-HAVE

Although the following tools and equipment aren't essentials, they can be pretty handy.

- JUICER. If you use a lot of fresh citrus fruit juices, this is nice to have. Look for wooden reamers, which make quick work of limes, lemons, and oranges.

- JULEP STRAINER. This type of strainer is designed to be used with a mixing glass, and is perfect for straining drinks with herbs. It is shaped like a satellite dish with holes in it.

- MICROPLANE. The Microplane is the industry standard for turning fruit peel and whole spices into tiny pieces.

- MORTAR AND PESTLE. This ancient tool, made out of granite, marble, or wood, is used for pounding herbs and spices.

- TEA STRAINER. If you want to double-strain your drinks, place one of these directly over the serving glass and pour the cocktail through.

GLASSWARE

The way a drink looks is just as important as the way it tastes. Having the right glassware will go a long way toward impressing your guests.

- CHAMPAGNE FLUTE. Average capacity: 6 to 8 ounces. A long, slender glass with a stem; good for cocktails that feature sparkling wine.

- COLLINS GLASS. Average capacity: 8 to 12 ounces. A skinnier version of the highball; the two are interchangeable.

- COUPE GLASS. Average capacity: 6 to 8 ounces. The wide, U-shaped vintage glass with a stem; for classic cocktails served without ice.

- HIGHBALL GLASS. Average capacity: 10 to 12 ounces. The tall, skinny version of a rocks glass; great for drinks with more liquid that are meant to be served over regular-size ice cubes or crushed ice.

- MARGARITA GLASS. Average capacity: 8 to 12 ounces. The classic bell-shaped glass with generous proportions and a stem.

- MARTINI GLASS. Average capacity: 5 to 6 ounces. The classic arrow-shaped glass with a stem; for classic cocktails served without ice cubes.

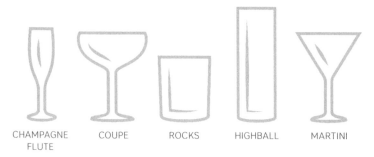

CHAMPAGNE FLUTE   COUPE   ROCKS   HIGHBALL   MARTINI

A Hangover Cure?

When it comes to hangovers, just as with the common cold, there are many remedies that alleviate symptoms, but a true cure remains elusive. A pounding headache, an extreme sensitivity to light and movement, a stomach that refuses to settle—these are the classic symptoms of a hangover, and most people, at one point or another, have had to endure one after a night of good times and good fun.

Well, luckily for you, there is one remedy worth trying that might actually work. Ask any New Orleans bartender about curing hangovers, and he or she will probably instruct you to do something like this.

- Pour 8 ounces of sparkling water into a highball glass. Add about 20 dashes of Angostura or Peychaud's bitters, or enough to turn the drink bright pink. Drink as quickly as possible—all at once if you can.

In about 15 minutes, you should be feeling better. If it works for the hard-partying folks who visit New Orleans year-round, it'll probably work for you, too. Why not give it a shot? After all, you've already got all the ingredients.

- ROCKS GLASS. Average capacity: singles, 6 to 8 ounces; doubles, 10 to 12 ounces. Look for a glass that has a nice weight and a sturdy base; great for drinks with less liquid that are meant to be served over large ice cubes.

- SNIFTER. Average capacity: 5 to 8 ounces. A bowl-shaped glass with a slightly narrowed top to concentrate aromas and a stem. Used for serving brandy. Not essential but nice to have.

THE METHOD

Now that you have all the ingredients and equipment, it's time to learn how to make bitters. There are two ways to make bitters: the combine and infuse method, and the tincture method.

COMBINE AND INFUSE

When using this method, you will combine all your bittering agents and flavoring agents in the liquor and infuse them together.

To combine and infuse, place the bittering agents, flavoring agents, and spirits in an appropriate-size jar and seal with the lid. Shake every day for two weeks. Then strain the agents from the spirits and blanch the agents in water. Let them sit apart for a week—the spirits in one jar, and the water (with the agents) in another. After that, discard the agents, and mix the spirits and water together with a touch of sweetener.

>> According to Eric Arnold in *The Booze Blog* of *Forbes* magazine, in New Orleans, bartenders are no strangers to first-time visitors to the city struggling with hangovers. Their go-to remedy is a glass of seltzer with a sizable dose of bitters. <<

This method is more beginner friendly and you won't need much in the way of glassware. The downside is that it can lack precision when it comes to the final taste profile. Because the aromas and flavors of some agents permeate the spirits faster than others, it can be tough to achieve balance. So you might end up with bitters that have too much of one flavor and not enough of another. It's a bit like using Neapolitan ice cream to make a milk shake.

TINCTURE

The tincture method combines single-agent solutions that have from 30 to 60 percent alcohol by volume, depending on the spirit used, to make bitters.

Creating bitters using this method is a two-step process: First you make separate tinctures (infuse spirit with agent) for the bittering and flavoring agents, and then you mix bittering and flavoring tinctures to develop a bespoke bitters.

After making the tinctures, you create bitters by adding the bittering and flavoring tinctures, one at a time, to a clean bowl, stirring well. Taste as you go, adjusting the amounts as you see fit. When you've got the right mix, dilute with water (if necessary) to reduce to 45 percent alcohol by volume.

There are three advantages to this method. First, it's precise; it's like using separate scoops of chocolate, vanilla, and strawberry ice cream to make a milkshake. And each tincture will have the maximum amount of aroma and flavor extracted from each ingredient.

Second, because every agent is kept separate during the infusion period, you'll gain greater understanding of how different agents smell and taste when they're done permeating the spirit, and how long they take.

Third and finally, you can create smaller batches of bitters and experiment. Unlike the combine and infuse method, you can effect flavor changes instantaneously, and if it isn't pleasing, you can throw out the whole thing and start over.

The downside? You'll need a ton of glassware.

TIPS FOR BETTER BITTERS

With the following parting tips in mind, you'll be well on your way to becoming a bitters master.

- INFUSE IN CLEAR GLASSWARE. This will make it easy to see color changes, which is especially useful when making tinctures.

- IT'S BATH TIME. Make sure agents are totally immersed in spirits.

- LABEL. For each container, write the main ingredients and date on the label.

A Bitters Tasting

One of the most challenging things when it comes to making bitters is learning how flavors will interact with each other. If you're an avid cook, you can draw on your kitchen experience; start with flavor pairings that are familiar and comfortable to you. But no matter what your skill level, it's useful to explore what different bittering agents taste like, because these ingredients are unfamiliar to most cooks and bartenders.

Start by smelling the ingredient, and write down the first descriptors that come to mind, drawing on your past food experiences.

Next, try brewing it like tea. Pour 1 cup of boiling water over a teaspoon of the agent, and let it steep for at least 5 minutes, or until fully flavored. Smell it, noting any differences in aroma when brewed, and take a sip. Rate the bitterness on a scale, and try to note any flavors beyond bitterness. Write down possible pairings with flavoring agents. Repeat this exercise whenever you purchase new bittering agents.

This way, you'll have a set of ideas you can try the next time you'd like to create your own bitters recipe.

Finally, taste your bitters once they're done. Professional bartenders vary in their methods. One method is to place a few drops on your wrist, rub them in, and smell them. Then place a drop or two in some seltzer and taste the result or, better yet, test-drive the bitters in a cocktail that works with the flavors in the bitters.

- THE LIGHT, IT BURNS! Always place the bottles away from direct sunlight to prevent oxidation.

- SHAKE IT UP TO WAKE IT UP. Agitating bottles and jars daily maximizes aroma and flavor.

- WELL, HELLO AGAIN. During the infusion process, place bottles and jars in a well-trafficked area, so that you remember to shake them. If you're using the tincture method, you can also monitor for color changes.

- FUNNELS ARE YOUR FRIEND. When transferring liquids, funnels prevent spillage.

- STORE IN DARK GLASSWARE. Dark bottles increase the shelf life of your bitters and tinctures.

- CHOP, BRUISE, OR CRUSH. Increasing the surface area of an agent exposes more of it to the spirit, and releases essential oils. Try it on herbs, fruit peels, nuts, and spices.

- TIME FOR A TOAST. Toasting nuts and spices before starting the infusion process intensifies their flavors.

Your Tincture Primer

As previously mentioned, there are two different ways to make bitters, the combine and infuse method and the tincture method. While infusing all of your ingredients together is often a simpler process, using tinctures can give you more accuracy and more room to experiment. The following chapters include recipes that use both methods, and this section will be your go-to resource for all tincture recipes. Here you'll find helpful instructions and tips for making tinctures, as well as the standard infusion times for every tincture you'll come across in the recipes to follow.

HOW TO MAKE A TINCTURE

To make a tincture, follow these simple steps:

1. Start with a clean glass jar. A 4-ounce glass jar works well.

2. Fill the jar with a high-proof spirit. You will get the most neutral flavor using high-proof vodka or Everclear, but you can also experiment with using high-proof bourbon, rye or rum.

3. Immerse the agent in the spirit using a ratio of 2 to 1 (spirit to agent) for fresh ingredients and 5 to 1 for dried ingredients.

4. Depending on the agent, a tincture can take just a few hours to be ready, or up to a month (see chart on following page).

5. When the tincture is ready, strain out the solids using a mesh strainer or coffee filter.

TIPS FOR MAKING TINCTURES

MAKE SEVERAL TINCTURES AT ONCE. You'll need several tinctures to make bitters, so it's worthwhile to make many tinctures at once. This way you'll have them on hand as you experiment with the recipes in this book and your own flavor combinations.

LABEL YOUR TINCTURES. When making several tinctures at once, it can be easy to forget what's what. Label each tincture with the agent and the date started.

MARK YOUR CALENDAR. Mark your calendar with the date your infusions are expected to finish. When you're making several tinctures with different infusion periods, it can be difficult to keep track of everything.

CHECK YOUR TINCTURES. Smell and taste your tinctures every couple of days. When the tincture is ready, the spirit will smell and taste strongly of the agent. A helpful way to taste the tincture is to pipe a little of the infusion into a glass of water.

TAKE NOTES. There is no tried-and-true formula for making tinctures. Write down the ratios you use and your infusion times as you experiment so that you can keep track of what works and what doesn't.

BITTERS BOTANICALS
AND THEIR STANDARD INFUSION PERIODS

The following chart outlines the standard infusion times for every tincture that you will find in the recipes in this book.

INGREDIENT	TIME (DAYS)	AGENT TYPE
Apple	24	Flavoring
Cardamom	10	Flavoring
Celery	29	Flavoring
Cinchona bark	29	Bittering
Cinnamon	10	Flavoring
Clove	10	Flavoring
Coconut flakes	24	Flavoring
Cucumber	27	Flavoring
Fennel seed	10	Flavoring
Gentian root	27	Bittering
Ginger	10	Flavoring
Horehound	29	Bittering
Lemon	15	Flavoring
Lime	15	Flavoring
Mint	10	Flavoring
Orange	12	Flavoring
Strawberry	10	Flavoring
Thyme	12	Flavoring

PART TWO

THE RECIPES

Winter is citrus's time to shine. The fruits reach peak flavor during this season, and more obscure varieties—such as Meyer lemon and blood orange—can be found only during the cold months. Winter is also time to take advantage of warm, inviting spices such as cardamom, distinctive winter herbs such as rosemary, and luxurious delicacies such as chocolate. With ingredients such as these, the prospect of staying indoors won't seem so limiting.

CHAPTER THREE

WINTER

ORANGE BITTERS

MAKES 10 OUNCES

Once upon a time, orange bitters were just as critical to making cocktails as heavyweights Peychaud's and Angostura are today. In fact, even in the wake of Prohibition, recipes for martinis continued to call for them. That's certainly one productive use of these versatile bitters, but try them in all manner of cocktails.

PREP TIME: 10 MINUTES   INFUSING TIME: 3½ WEEKS

¼ cup chopped Dried Orange
   Peel (see page 75)
3 cardamom pods, crushed
1 (1-inch) piece ginger,
   peeled and julienned
½ teaspoon cinchona bark

1 cup high-proof vodka
   or grain alcohol
½ cup water
1 tablespoon Rich Syrup
   (see facing page)

1. In a clean, clear glass jar with a tight-fitting lid, combine the dried orange peel, cardamom, ginger, cinchona bark, and vodka and seal with the lid. Make sure that the agents are completely submerged in the liquid.

2. Shake to combine and place in a well-trafficked area away from direct sunlight.

3. For 2 weeks, agitate the jar daily.

4. Place a snug-fitting funnel over another clean, clear glass jar. Line it with cheesecloth and strain the mixture, reserving the agents. Seal with the lid and place away from direct sunlight.

5. Transfer the agents to a saucepan and cover with the water.

6. Bring to a boil, then reduce to a simmer and cover with a lid; cook for 10 minutes.

7. Remove from the heat, let cool to room temperature, transfer to another clean, clear glass jar, and seal with the lid.

8. Shake to combine and place in a well-trafficked area away from direct sunlight.

9. For 1 week, agitate the jar daily.

10. Place a snug-fitting funnel over another clean, clear glass jar. Line it with cheesecloth and strain the liquid, discarding the agents.

11. Add this liquid and the syrup to the vodka solution and shake to combine.

12. Wait 3 days before using, or until any floaters come to the top.

13. Place a snug-fitting funnel over another clean, clear glass jar. Line it with cheesecloth and strain the mixture, discarding any floaters.

14. Transfer to smaller, dark-colored bottles using a funnel.

TIP: Placing the jars in a well-trafficked area will remind you to check on your bitters regularly.

Rich Syrup

MAKES 1½ CUPS

2 cups raw sugar
1 cup water

1. In a medium saucepan, combine the sugar and water and bring to a simmer over medium heat.

2. Stir gently until the sugar is dissolved.

3. Let cool to room temperature, and transfer to an airtight container. Rich syrup will keep in the refrigerator for up to 1 month.

RIVEREDGE COCKTAIL, SHAKEN UP

MAKES 1 DRINK

James Beard was the creator of the original version of this recipe, which was a blended drink. This reimagined take is shaken and served up, making the cocktail much more winter friendly. It's a great way to take advantage of the bounty of citrus available at this time of year.

PREP TIME: 5 MINUTES

2 ounces gin
1 ounce dry vermouth
1 ounce freshly squeezed
   orange juice

3 dashes Orange Bitters (page 50)
   or Regan's Orange Bitters No. 6
1 strip orange zest, for garnish
½ orange wheel, for garnish

1. Fill a shaker two-thirds full with ice, and fill a martini glass with ice water.

2. Add the gin, vermouth, orange juice, and bitters to the shaker.

3. Shake for 10 to 15 seconds, or until chilled.

4. Discard the ice water, strain into the martini glass, and serve garnished with the orange zest and orange wheel.

TIP: On average, one juice orange contains 2 ½ to 3 ounces of juice.

PORT MARGARITA

MAKES 1 DRINK

Think that just because it's winter you can't have a margarita?
Think again. Peter Vestinos, the award-winning bartender who
helped spearhead Chicago's cocktail revolution at the Michelin-
starred restaurant Sepia, developed this recipe for the Wirtz
Beverage Group.

PREP TIME: 5 MINUTES

2 ounces tequila, such as Avión
¾ ounce port, such as Sandeman
    Porto Founders Reserve
¾ ounce freshly squeezed lime juice

¼ ounce agave nectar
1 dash Orange Bitters (page 50),
    or Regan's Orange Bitters No. 6
1 lime wheel, for garnish

1. Fill a shaker two-thirds full with ice, and fill a rocks glass
   with ice.

2. Add the tequila, port, lime juice, agave nectar, and bitters to
   the shaker.

3. Shake for 10 to 15 seconds, or until chilled.

4. Strain into the rocks glass and serve garnished with the
   lime wheel.

   TIP: Agave nectar is a sweetener that can be found next to
   the maple syrup in the baking aisle of the supermarket.

ROSEMARY BITTERS

MAKES 10 OUNCES

Rosemary evokes memories of cozy winters—braised leg of lamb, roasted potatoes, and rosemary focaccia come to mind. It brings a luxurious touch to comfort foods, and can do the same for cocktails by adding a welcoming savory element. Try using rosemary bitters to spruce up gin-based drinks or cocktails featuring citrus or pear.

PREP TIME: 5 MINUTES   INFUSING TIME: 3½ WEEKS

2 rosemary sprigs, stemmed and coarsely chopped
Zest of 1 lemon
½ teaspoon horehound

1 cup high-proof vodka or grain alcohol
½ cup water
1 tablespoon honey

1. In a clean, clear glass jar with a tight-fitting lid, combine the rosemary, lemon zest, horehound, and vodka and seal with the lid. Make sure that the agents are completely submerged in the liquid.

2. Shake to combine and place in a well-trafficked area away from direct sunlight.

3. For 2 weeks, agitate the jar daily.

4. Place a snug-fitting funnel over another clean, clear glass jar. Line it with cheesecloth and strain the mixture, reserving the agents. Seal with the lid and place away from direct sunlight.

5. Transfer the agents to a saucepan, and cover with the water.

6. Bring to a boil, then reduce to a simmer and cover with a lid; cook for 10 minutes.

7. Remove from the heat, let cool to room temperature, transfer to another clean, clear glass jar, and seal with the lid.

8. Shake to combine and place in a well-trafficked area away from direct sunlight.

9. For 1 week, agitate the jar daily.

10. Place a snug-fitting funnel over another clean, clear glass jar. Line it with cheesecloth and strain the liquid, discarding the agents.

11. Add this liquid and the honey to the vodka solution and shake to combine.

12. Wait 3 days before using, or until any floaters come to the top.

13. Place a snug-fitting funnel over another clean, clear glass jar. Line it with cheesecloth and strain the mixture, discarding any floaters.

14. Transfer to smaller, dark-colored bottles using a funnel.

TIP: Placing the jars in an area away from direct sunlight will prevent the ingredients oxidizing.

ROSEMARY GREYHOUND

MAKES 1 DRINK

The Bloody Mary, Mimosa, and even the Bellini all get a lot more love and attention than the humble Greyhound during the typical boozy Sunday brunch. That's too bad, because it was never in need of a huge makeover, just a few updates here and there. Made with care (read: freshly squeezed juice) and a touch of rosemary bitters, it's all set for a comeback.

PREP TIME: 1 MINUTE

2 ounces vodka
3 dashes Rosemary Bitters
  (page 54)

3 ounces freshly squeezed
  grapefruit juice
1 rosemary sprig, for garnish

1. Fill a highball glass or Collins glass half full with ice.

2. In the following order, add the vodka, bitters, and grapefruit juice.

3. Using a bar spoon, stir a few times and serve garnished with the rosemary sprig.

TIP: On average, one grapefruit contains 6 ounces of juice.

RITZ BIJOU

MAKES 1 DRINK

A look at the ingredients for the original version of this cocktail—crystal-clear gin, ruby-red sweet vermouth, and emerald-green Chartreuse—makes it apparent where the inspiration for the name came from. (*Bijou* means "jewel" in French.) But the original version has been criticized for being too sweet, and so this recipe, inspired by the Ritz version in Frank Meier's book *The Artistry of Mixing Drinks*, makes a few substitutions in an improvement on the original.

PREP TIME: 5 MINUTES

2 ounces gin
1 ounce dry vermouth
½ ounce triple sec

3 dashes Rosemary Bitters (page 54)
1 small rosemary sprig, for garnish

1. Fill a mixing glass two-thirds full with ice, and fill a martini glass with ice water.

2. Add the gin, vermouth, triple sec, and bitters to the mixing glass.

3. Using a bar spoon, stir for 30 seconds, or until chilled.

4. Discard the ice water, strain into the martini glass, and serve garnished with the rosemary sprig.

   TIP: To chill the martini glass even more quickly, fill it with ice and leave it under a gently running faucet while you make the cocktail.

BLOOD ORANGE BITTERS

MAKES 10 OUNCES

Few things chase away the winter blues like cutting into a juicy, ripe blood orange. The seductive color of the blood orange is matched by a deep citrus flavor that takes well to warm, bold spices such as cinnamon. Compared with regular orange bitters, blood orange bitters stand up better to spirits that have equally bold flavors such as brandy, rye, or Scotch. They can also bring balance to cocktails that include sweet vermouth or sweet liqueurs such as triple sec.

PREP TIME: 10 MINUTES

INFUSING TIME: $3\frac{1}{2}$ WEEKS

¼ cup chopped Dried Blood Orange Peel (see page 75)
1 cinnamon stick
1 (1-inch) piece ginger, peeled and julienned

½ teaspoon cinchona bark
1 cup high-proof rye whiskey
½ cup water
1 tablespoon blackstrap molasses

1. In a clean, clear glass jar with a tight-fitting lid, combine the dried blood orange peel, cinnamon stick, ginger, cinchona bark, and rye, and seal with the lid. Make sure that the agents are completely submerged in the liquid.

2. Shake to combine and place in a well-trafficked area away from direct sunlight.

3. For 2 weeks, agitate the jar daily.

4. Place a snug-fitting funnel over another clean, clear glass jar. Line it with cheesecloth and strain the mixture, reserving the agents. Seal with the lid and place away from direct sunlight.

5. Transfer the agents to a saucepan and cover with the water.

6. Bring to a boil, then reduce to a simmer and cover with a lid; cook for 10 minutes.

7. Remove from the heat, let cool to room temperature, transfer to another clean, clear glass jar, and seal with the lid.

8. Shake to combine and place in a well-trafficked area away from direct sunlight.

9. For 1 week, agitate the jar daily.

10. Place a snug-fitting funnel over another clean, clear glass jar. Line it with cheesecloth and strain the liquid, discarding the agents.

11. Add this liquid and the molasses to the rye solution and shake to combine.

12. Wait 3 days before using, or until any floaters come to the top.

13. Place a snug-fitting funnel over another clean, clear glass jar. Line it with cheesecloth and strain the mixture, discarding any floaters.

14. Transfer to smaller, dark-colored bottles using a funnel.

TIP: Side vegetable peelers make quick work of peeling fresh ginger.

BLOODY FRENCH CONNECTION

MAKES 1 DRINK

In the middle of the Bois de Boulogne on a snowy Paris evening, a clandestine meeting goes wrong—such was the inspiration behind this cocktail. Well, not really. The classic French Connection, a simple stirred concoction of Cognac and Grand Marnier, marries well with the bold flavor of blood oranges, the true reference for the name of this cocktail. Feel free to tell your guests otherwise.

Most recipes for the French Connection cocktail call for only two ingredients, which, if you were to ask Peggy Olson (see page 11), would qualify as an emergency. Maybe it is. But it's still a far cry from vodka and Mountain Dew.

PREP TIME: 5 MINUTES

2 ounces Cognac
1 ounce Grand Marnier
3 dashes Blood Orange
  Bitters (page 58)

1 strip blood orange
  zest, for garnish

1. Fill a mixing glass two-thirds full with ice, and fill a martini glass with ice water.

2. Add the Cognac, Grand Marnier, and bitters to the mixing glass.

3. Using a bar spoon, stir for 30 seconds, or until chilled.

4. Discard the ice water, strain into the martini glass, and serve garnished with the blood orange zest.

TIP: Twist citrus peels to release essential oils, and rub over the rim of the glass to add extra citrus flavor to every sip.

BLOOD ORANGE NEGRONI

MAKES 1 DRINK

The Negroni—the iconic Italian aperitif—has been making a quiet comeback in the wake of the cocktail renaissance. As originally conceived, the cocktail does make use of bitters—Campari—albeit the potable type once used in Europe as medicine. Whatever cocktail book you look in, if it is decent, will have the same exact ratios used here so, rightfully, they haven't been altered. But with a few dashes of homemade blood orange bitters, you can make a classic your own.

PREP TIME: 1 MINUTE

1½ ounces Campari
1½ ounces sweet vermouth
1½ ounces gin

3 dashes Blood Orange
Bitters (page 58)
½ blood orange wheel, for garnish

1. Fill a rocks glass half full with ice.

2. In the following order, add the Campari, vermouth, gin, and bitters.

3. Using a bar spoon, stir a few times and serve garnished with the blood orange wheel.

CHOCOLATE BITTERS

MAKES 10 OUNCES

Chocolate is a delicious sweet any time of year, but as a cocktail ingredient, it seems to make the most sense during the winter. After all, whether it's raining hard or snowing where you live, a boozy hot chocolate sounds enticing. But that—along with dessert cocktails in general—is a no-brainer, and so you'll have a chance to experiment with those types of drinks in the section at the end of the chapter, "Take It to the Next Level" (see page 76), as a homework assignment. For now, in the next two recipes, you'll experience what chocolate bitters can do outside the realm of dessert drinks.

PREP TIME: 1 MINUTE   INFUSING TIME: 3½ WEEKS

¼ cup cacao nibs
1 vanilla bean, split
1 cinnamon stick
¼ teaspoon wormwood

1 cup high-proof bourbon
½ cup water
1 tablespoon Rich Syrup (page 51)

1. In a clean, clear glass jar with a tight-fitting lid, combine the cacao nibs, vanilla bean, cinnamon stick, wormwood, and bourbon, and seal with the lid. Make sure that the agents are completely submerged in the liquid.

2. Shake to combine and place in a well-trafficked area away from direct sunlight.

3. For 2 weeks, agitate the jar daily.

4. Place a snug-fitting funnel over another clean, clear glass jar. Line it with cheesecloth and strain the mixture, reserving the agents. Seal with the lid and place away from direct sunlight.

5. Transfer the agents to a saucepan and cover with the water.

6. Bring to a boil, then reduce to a simmer and cover with a lid; cook for 10 minutes.

7. Remove from the heat, let cool to room temperature, transfer to another clean, clear glass jar, and seal with the lid.

8. Shake to combine and place in a well-trafficked area away from direct sunlight.

9. For 1 week, agitate the jar daily.

10. Place a snug-fitting funnel over another clean, clear glass jar. Line it with cheesecloth and strain the liquid, discarding the agents.

11. Add this liquid and the syrup to the bourbon solution and shake to combine.

12. Wait 3 days before using, or until any floaters come to the top.

13. Place a snug-fitting funnel over another clean, clear glass jar. Line it with cheesecloth and strain the mixture, discarding any floaters.

14. Transfer to smaller, dark-colored bottles using a funnel.

TIP: If you can't find cacao nibs, look for 100 percent cacao baking bars. A 2-ounce bar, finely chopped, will work nicely.

A DARK DAY ON BROADWAY

MAKES 1 DRINK

When the lights go out on Broadway and the wind's blowing hard, the warm embrace of Scotch whiskey sounds inviting. For the uninitiated, though, the prospect of a Scotch-based drink may sound a bit daunting; Scotch, after all, can have very assertive flavors.

Well, this cocktail may change your mind: The combination of sweet vermouth and maraschino liqueur tames Scotch into a velvety smooth spirit, while chocolate bitters keep the sweetness in check. The result? An amber drink that doesn't taste like an amber drink.

PREP TIME: 5 MINUTES

1 ounce blended Scotch whiskey, such as The Black Grouse
1½ ounces sweet vermouth
½ ounce maraschino liqueur
3 dashes Chocolate Bitters (page 62)
1 maraschino cherry, for garnish

1. Fill a mixing glass two-thirds full with ice, and fill a martini glass with ice water.

2. Add the Scotch, vermouth, maraschino liqueur, and bitters to the mixing glass.

3. Using a bar spoon, stir for 30 seconds, or until chilled.

4. Discard the ice water, strain into the martini glass, and serve garnished with the cherry.

SMOKY OLD FASHIONED

MAKES 1 DRINK

Are you a master of the classic version and looking for a challenge? Or perhaps it's your favorite cocktail, and you're looking for a twist. Then this recipe from Alex Mendelsohn, partner at Orale Mexican Kitchen in Jersey City, New Jersey, is definitely worth a try.

PREP TIME: 15 MINUTES

1 orange wheel
1 (10-ounce jar) maraschino
    cherries, in syrup
1 ounce bourbon, such
    as Old Grand-Dad
½ ounce mezcal, such as
    Del Maguey Vida
½ ounce nectarine-flavored
    vodka, such as 44° North

¼ ounce sweet vermouth,
    such as Carpano Antica
2 dashes Chocolate Bitters
    (page 62), or Bittermens
    Xocolatl Mole Bitters
1 drop liquid smoke,
    preferably organic

1. Using a butane torch, torch the orange wheel and place in a snifter or rocks glass with 1 large ice cube.

2. Put 3 cherries in a mixing glass and mash lightly using the flat end of a muddler.

3. Add the bourbon, mezcal, vodka, vermouth, bitters, and liquid smoke. Fill with ice until two-thirds full and stir for 45 seconds, or until well chilled.

4. Strain into the serving glass.

GRAPEFRUIT BITTERS

MAKES 6¼ OUNCES

Grapefruit bitters, like orange bitters, are at home with gin-based cocktails, and also play well with light rum and tequila blanco. Here, grapefruit is combined with mint for a hint of herbal sweetness to balance out its natural tartness. You can use white or red grapefruit peels to make the tinctures; just make sure to buy whatever looks fresh.

Create the tinctures required for this recipe using the procedure outlined in chapter 2 (see sidebar, "Your Tincture Primer," page 44).

PREP TIME: 1 MINUTE   INFUSING TIME: 29 DAYS

3 ounces grapefruit tincture
½ ounce cinchona bark tincture
½ ounce mint tincture

2 ounces water
¼ ounce Rich Syrup (page 51)

1. In a clean bowl, combine the grapefruit, cinchona bark, and mint tinctures and mix thoroughly.

2. Add the water and syrup and, using a funnel, transfer to dark-colored bottles.

TIP: Tinctures are ready when they smell strongly of the bittering or flavoring ingredient. If they still smell like alcohol, they need more time.

GINGER-GRAPEFRUIT
GIN & TONIC

MAKES 1 DRINK

Does your usual pick-me-up feel like it's in need of, well, a pick-me-up? Ryan Lynch McEnerney, creator of the Gin & Tonic Program at Raval Tapas Bar and Cocktail Lounge in Jersey City, New Jersey, shares one of his favorites. He's a fan of the Bittermens product, but feel free to use your very own grapefruit bitters.

PREP TIME: 5 MINUTES

2 ounces gin, such as Barr Hill
   Tom Cat Barrel-Aged
1 ounce freshly squeezed
   grapefruit juice

6 drops Grapefruit Bitters
   (page 66), or Bittermens
   Hopped Grapefruit Bitters
2 ounces ginger beer
1 small grapefruit wedge,
   for garnish

1. Fill a mixing glass two-thirds full with ice, and fill a highball glass half full with ice.

2. Add the gin, grapefruit juice, and bitters to the mixing glass.

3. Using a bar spoon, stir for 30 seconds, or until chilled.

4. Strain into the highball glass and add the ginger beer.

5. Stir lightly and serve garnished with the grapefruit wedge.

GRAPEFRUIT CHANTICLEER

MAKES 1 DRINK

The Chanticleer was a popular cocktail at the old Waldorf-Astoria, where the optional garnish was a coxcomb from a rooster. (The name is French; *chanticleer* translates as "rooster.") The egg white in the drink, when shaken, creates a smooth foam at the top that gives it a luxurious touch.

This version of the drink takes things in a slightly different direction from the original with the addition of freshly squeezed grapefruit juice and grapefruit bitters.

PREP TIME: 5 MINUTES

1½ ounces gin
1½ ounces dry vermouth
½ ounce triple sec
½ ounce freshly squeezed
 grapefruit juice

1 large egg white
3 dashes Grapefruit Bitters (page 66)
1 strip grapefruit zest, for garnish

1. Fill a shaker two-thirds full with ice, and fill a rocks glass with ice water.

2. Add the gin, vermouth, triple sec, grapefruit juice, egg white, and bitters to the shaker.

3. Shake for 10 to 15 seconds, or until chilled.

4. Discard the ice water, strain into the rocks glass, and serve garnished with the grapefruit zest.

CARDAMOM BITTERS

MAKES 5¾ OUNCES

Cardamom is a spice that is a key ingredient in Indian, North African, and Middle Eastern cooking. The teardrop-shaped pods—which come in green, black, or white varieties—contain seeds that carry the majority of the flavor and aroma, at once both citrusy and savory.

Use these bitters to add a burst of freshness to cocktails that might otherwise lean sweet or boozy (such as the Old Fashioned), or to complement ones with citrus accents (such as gin-based cocktails).

Create the tinctures required for this recipe using the procedure outlined in chapter 2 (see sidebar, "Your Tincture Primer," page 44).

PREP TIME: 10 MINUTES   INFUSING TIME: 29 DAYS

2½ ounces cardamom tincture
½ ounce cinchona bark tincture
½ ounce ginger tincture

2 ounces water
¼ ounce Rich Syrup (page 51)

1. In a clean bowl, combine the cardamom, cinchona bark, and ginger tinctures and mix thoroughly.

2. Add the water and syrup and, using a funnel, transfer to dark-colored bottles.

OLD FASHIONED

MAKES 1 DRINK

Bobby Gleason, master mixologist for Beam Suntory, shares a recipe for a modern take on the Old Fashioned cocktail. Angostura bitters are the usual choice, but if you've made your own cardamom bitters, they're definitely worth a shot, too.

To make the classic version, substitute rye whiskey for the bourbon and omit the cherry and orange; serve garnished with a lemon peel.

PREP TIME: 5 MINUTES

1 sugar cube
2 dashes Cardamom Bitters
   (page 69), or Angostura bitters
1 maraschino cherry

½ orange wheel
2 ounces bourbon,
   such as Jim Beam White
1 orange slice, for garnish

1. Place the sugar cube in a rocks glass and soak with the bitters.

2. Add the cherry and orange.

3. Using the flat end of a muddler, mash the ingredients until the sugar cube dissolves completely.

4. Fill the glass half full with ice, and then add the bourbon.

5. Stir for 30 seconds, or until well chilled.

6. Serve garnished with the orange slice.

RYE BUCK

Here's a cocktail that features winter ingredients with a decidedly breezy attitude. This recipe comes from Amy Fahland, restaurant manager at Sansei Seafood Restaurant & Sushi Bar, located in Kapalua, Hawaii. She uses Angostura bitters in her restaurant, but cardamom bitters also play well with the flavors of ginger and lime in the cocktail.

PREP TIME: 1 MINUTE

1¼ ounces rye whiskey, such as Old Overholt
1¼ ounces ginger beer
1 dash Cardamom Bitters (page 69), or Angostura bitters

1 ounce freshly squeezed lime juice
3 ounces sparkling water
1 lime wedge, for garnish

1. In the following order, add the rye, ginger beer, bitters, lime juice, and sparkling water to a highball glass.

2. Add ice and, using a bar spoon, stir a few times.

3. Serve garnished with the lime wedge.

ORANGE-FENNEL BITTERS

MAKES 6¼ OUNCES

Fennel and orange are a natural match. The sweet, licorice-y flavor of fennel contrasts nicely with the refreshing acidity of oranges in this versatile bitters recipe, which draws upon the most forward flavors in Peychaud's bitters as inspiration. Feel free to use this basic recipe as a jumping-off point, and experiment with your own additions.

Create the tinctures required for this recipe using the procedure outlined in chapter 2 (see sidebar, "Your Tincture Primer," page 44).

PREP TIME: 1 MINUTE   INFUSING TIME: 29 DAYS

3 ounces orange tincture
½ ounce cinchona bark tincture
½ ounce fennel seed tincture

2 ounces water
¼ ounce Rich Syrup (page 51)

1. In a clean bowl, combine the orange, cinchona bark, and fennel seed tinctures and mix thoroughly.

2. Add the water and syrup and, using a funnel, transfer to dark-colored bottles.

SAZERAC

Here it is: one of the most famed cocktails of New Orleans. Though no one person can be credited with its creation—see "You Think You Know—Sazerac" (page 25)—it's fair to say that it wouldn't exist without the work of Antoine Peychaud, a pharmacist from Haiti who created the bitters that have remained the foundation of the cocktail. If you've made your own orange-fennel bitters, it's a useful exercise to see how its flavor compares with that of Peychaud's.

PREP TIME: 5 MINUTES

1 sugar cube
3 dashes Orange-Fennel Bitters
    (page 72), or Peychaud's bitters

1½ ounces rye whiskey or bourbon
¼ ounce Herbsaint
1 strip lemon zest

1. Fill a rocks glass with ice.

2. Place the sugar cube in another rocks glass and soak with the bitters.

3. Using the flat end of a muddler, mash the sugar cube until it dissolves completely.

4. Add the rye.

5. Discard the ice from the first glass, and coat with the Herbsaint; discard any excess.

6. Pour the contents of the second glass into the first glass, and serve garnished with the lemon zest.

ACCIDENTAL CITY

MAKES 1 DRINK

James Ives, lead bartender for Pine at the Hanover Inn Dartmouth, a historic hotel owned by Dartmouth College in Hanover, New Hampshire, creates "restoration cocktails," classic drinks updated for modern tastes with premium liquors, infusions, bitters, and other interesting accents.

Ives says, "This sophisticated sipper in the style of a Sazerac is named for the book by historian Lawrence Powell about the founding of New Orleans." Ives's recipe calls for Peychaud's bitters, but if you've made your own orange-fennel bitters, they also work nicely in this cocktail.

PREP TIME: 5 MINUTES

¼ ounce absinthe or absinthe substitute, such as Herbsaint
1¼ ounces rye whiskey, preferably Bulleit
¾ ounce Armagnac, such as Marie Duffau

¼ ounce Bénédictine
1 teaspoon Rich Syrup (page 51)
3 dashes Orange-Fennel Bitters (page 72), or Peychaud's bitters
1 lemon peel

1. Coat a double rocks glass with the absinthe and discard the excess.

2. In a mixing glass, combine the rye, Armagnac, Bénédictine, syrup, and bitters.

3. Add ice to the level of the liquid in the mixing glass and stir for 49 revolutions.

4. Strain into the rocks glass, twist the lemon peel over the glass, trace the rim of the glass with the peel, and drop it in.

Make Your Own
Dried Orange Peel

Dried orange peel is a common ingredient in bitters. By evaporating the moisture present in the peels, you concentrate aromatic oils, which carry the flavor and aroma. This will give your bitters an extra punch that you just couldn't get by using fresh citrus peels.

Although you can find these store-bought, they aren't too difficult to make at home, which is much more economical. It's also worth noting that this procedure works for all kinds of citrus. And if you're already spending a few weeks making bitters, why not take a little more time to make your own dried orange peel as well?

1. Preheat the oven to 150°F, or as low as your oven will go.

2. Using a vegetable peeler, peel long strips from the fruit, taking care to remove only the colored part of the peel and leaving behind the white pith.

3. Lay them out in a single layer on a baking sheet.

4. Place in the oven for 45 minutes, or until the peels have thinned out and shrunk.

5. Remove from the oven, let cool, and store in a container covered with a lid.

Because you'll be extracting the peel's flavors into your bitters, it's a good idea to buy organic citrus. And it goes almost without saying, wash your fruit before getting started. Even organic produce sometimes has food-grade beeswax applied to it.

Take It to the Next Level

Now that you've gotten a taste of what it's like to work some of winter's best ingredients into familiar (and not-so-familiar) cocktails, it's time to branch out and come up with your own creations. Winter certainly has a lot more to offer than the small (but wonderful) set of fruits, herbs, and spices covered in this chapter. To help you get started brainstorming, here are more ideas for bitters, cocktails, and pairings that you can try as an exercise.

GO NUTS. Almonds, hazelnuts, pistachios, and walnuts are all great candidates as flavoring agents for bitters. They have complementary counterparts in the liqueur aisle that are key ingredients in classic winter cocktails, making them a natural choice for your next step. Be sure to buy them unsalted. Pre-roasted nuts have great flavor, but if you buy nuts raw and roast them yourself, you can save money on a pricey ingredient.

BITTERING AGENTS. Sweet, rich nuts, such as almonds, hazelnuts, or pistachios, play well with orris root or horehound, while bolder nuts, such as pecans or walnuts, can stand up to wormwood.

DON'T FORGET THE BAR. To complement your next homemade batch of nutty bitters, pick up bottles of the following:

- AMARETTO. An almond-flavored liqueur made by DiSaronno.

- CRÈME DE CACAO. Chocolate-flavored liqueur; available in light and dark varieties.

- FRANGELICO. A liqueur flavored with a proprietary blend of hazelnuts and herbs.

- KAHLÚA. A coffee-flavored liqueur.

TIME TO PLAY. Okay, now it's time for a homework assignment. Here is a list of cocktails worth seeking out, along with their key spirit and liqueur components and suggested bitters. Take notes on what works for you and what doesn't; everyone's flavor preferences are personal.

- **ALEXANDER.** Gin, white crème de cacao, pistachio bitters.

- **AMARETTO ALEXANDER.** Amaretto, white crème de cacao, almond bitters.

- **AMARETTO SOUR.** Amaretto, almond bitters.

- **BRANDY ALEXANDER.** Brandy, dark crème de cacao, walnut bitters.

- **BURNISHED GOLD.** Cognac, Frangelico, hazelnut bitters.

- **CHOCOLATE MARTINI.** Vodka, white crème de cacao, chocolate bitters.

- **GODFATHER.** Scotch, amaretto, almond bitters.

- **ITALIAN COFFEE.** Frangelico or amaretto, hazelnut or almond bitters, coffee.

- **TOASTED ALMOND.** Amaretto, Kahlúa, almond bitters.

- **WHITE RUSSIAN.** Vodka, Kahlúa, hazelnut bitters.

Spring is a time of dramatic transformation: The days get longer and warmer, the leaves return to the trees, and the farmers' market begins to bustle with activity again. The produce stands are dominated by fresh herbs, sprouts, and other leafy greens. You also start to see some of the first strawberries of the season, always an exciting time.

CHAPTER FOUR

SPRING

RHUBARB BITTERS

MAKES 10 OUNCES

The nickname for rhubarb may be pie plant, but that doesn't mean it should be confined to the realm of desserts. Rhubarb also works well in cocktails. Its tart flavor pairs nicely with orange zest, and a touch of herbal sweetness from mint and spiciness from fresh ginger keep the overall flavor of these bitters balanced.

PREP TIME: 10 MINUTES   INFUSING TIME: 3½ WEEKS

½ cup finely chopped rhubarb
Zest of ½ orange
¼ cup mint leaves
1 (1-inch) piece ginger,
    peeled and julienned

½ teaspoon cinchona bark
1 cup high-proof vodka
    or grain alcohol
½ cup water
1 tablespoon Rich Syrup (page 51)

1. In a clean, clear glass jar with a tight-fitting lid, combine the rhubarb, orange zest, mint, ginger, cinchona bark, and vodka and seal with the lid. Make sure that the agents are completely submerged in the liquid.

2. Shake to combine and place in a well-trafficked area away from direct sunlight.

3. For 2 weeks, agitate the jar daily.

4. Place a snug-fitting funnel over another clean, clear glass jar. Line it with cheesecloth and strain the mixture, reserving the agents. Seal with the lid and place away from direct sunlight.

5. Transfer the agents to a saucepan and cover with the water.

6. Bring to a boil, then reduce to a simmer and cover with a lid; cook for 10 minutes.

7. Remove from the heat, let cool to room temperature, transfer to another clean, clear glass jar, and seal with the lid.

8. Shake to combine and place in a well-trafficked area away from direct sunlight.

9. For 1 week, agitate the jar daily.

10. Place a snug-fitting funnel over another clean, clear glass jar. Line it with cheesecloth and strain the liquid, discarding the agents.

11. Add this liquid and the syrup to the vodka solution and shake to combine.

12. Wait 3 days before using, or until any floaters come to the top.

13. Place a snug-fitting funnel over another clean, clear glass jar. Line it with cheesecloth and strain the mixture, discarding any floaters.

14. Transfer to smaller, dark-colored bottles using a funnel.

TIP: When buying rhubarb, choose stalks that are bright red and sturdy; avoid ones that are limp or browning at the edges.

RHUBARB MARTINI

MAKES 1 DRINK

If historical accounts are accurate, martinis began as an off-shoot of the Manhattan in the late 19th century, when people asked bartenders to use gin instead of whiskey. It was a much sweeter drink than the modern-day version, made with gin, sweet vermouth, and even maraschino liqueur (which is very sweet), while orange bitters kept everything in balance.

Maraschino liqueur might not return to the martini anytime soon, but adding a dash or two of bitters could change your idea of just how good a martini can be. Here, rhubarb bitters herald the coming of spring.

PREP TIME: 5 MINUTES

2 ounces gin or vodka
1 ounce dry vermouth

3 dashes Rhubarb Bitters (page 80)
1 strip lemon zest, for garnish

1. Fill a mixing glass two-thirds full with ice, and fill a martini glass with ice water.

2. In the mixing glass, combine the gin, vermouth, and bitters.

3. Using a bar spoon, stir for 30 seconds, or until chilled.

4. Discard the ice water, strain into the martini glass, and serve garnished with the lemon zest.

TIP: Avoid refrigerating the spirits for a martini (or any similarly high-proof drink); doing so would prevent the ice from melting while you stir the drink. Without enough ice melting, the drink would taste too strong.

SANSEI MARTINEZ

MAKES 1 DRINK

The Martinez is the precursor to the dry martini, which dates back to 1887 when it made its appearance in Jerry Thomas's *How to Mix Drinks*. It called for more vermouth than gin, which resulted in a drink that some might consider sweet.

Amy Fahland, restaurant manager at Sansei Seafood Restaurant & Sushi Bar in Kapalua, Hawaii, gives a spring twist to the drink by adding a couple of dashes of rhubarb bitters. She stays true to the classic by using sweetened gin, but if you're using regular gin, substitute sweet vermouth for the dry.

PREP TIME: 5 MINUTES

2 ounces sweetened
(Old Tom–style) gin
½ ounce dry vermouth,
such as Dolin

½ ounce maraschino liqueur
2 dashes Rhubarb Bitters (page 80)

1. Fill a mixing glass two-thirds full with ice, and fill a martini glass with ice water.

2. In the mixing glass, combine the gin, vermouth, maraschino liqueur, and bitters.

3. Using a bar spoon, stir for 30 seconds, or until chilled.

4. Discard the ice water, strain into the martini glass, and serve immediately.

TIP: To stir a drink using a bar spoon, grab the corkscrew-shaped portion in the center using your index finger, middle finger, and thumb, and use your wrist to make a smooth circular motion. It can take some time to develop this skill, so don't feel bad if you don't get the hang of it for a while. Watching videos online definitely helps, and patience is key.

LEMONGRASS BITTERS

MAKES 10 OUNCES

Mcson Salicetti, former bartender at the Black Ant in New York City, came up with this versatile bitters recipe, which showcases one of spring's most overlooked ingredients: lemongrass. Although it is available year-round, lemongrass reaches peak flavor in the spring. Its exotic citrus aroma adds a refreshing twist to your favorite cocktails.

PREP TIME: 1 MINUTE   INFUSING TIME: 3½ WEEKS

---

6 teaspoons chopped lemongrass
4 teaspoons chopped lemon peel
1 teaspoon chopped Kaffir
  lime leaves
1 teaspoon gentian
½ teaspoon wormwood

½ teaspoon cardamom seeds
½ teaspoon whole coriander seeds
1 cup high-proof vodka
  or grain alcohol
½ cup water

1. In a clean, clear glass jar with a tight-fitting lid, combine the lemongrass, lemon peel, Kaffir lime leaves, gentian, wormwood, cardamom, coriander, and vodka and seal with the lid. Make sure that the agents are completely submerged in the liquid.

2. Shake to combine and place in a well-trafficked area away from direct sunlight.

3. For 2 weeks, agitate the jar daily.

4. Place a snug-fitting funnel over another clean, clear glass jar. Line it with cheesecloth and strain the mixture, reserving the agents. Seal with the lid and place away from direct sunlight.

5. Transfer the agents to a saucepan and cover with the water.

6. Bring to a boil, then reduce to a simmer and cover with a lid; cook for 10 minutes.

7. Remove from the heat, let cool to room temperature, transfer to another clean, clear glass jar, and seal with the lid.

8. Shake to combine and place in a well-trafficked area away from direct sunlight.

9. For 1 week, agitate the jar daily.

10. Place a snug-fitting funnel over another clean, clear glass jar. Line it with cheesecloth and strain the liquid, discarding the agents.

11. Add this liquid to the vodka solution and shake to combine.

12. Wait 3 days before using, or until any floaters come to the top.

13. Place a snug-fitting funnel over another clean, clear glass jar. Line it with cheesecloth and strain the mixture, discarding any floaters.

14. Transfer to smaller, dark-colored bottles using a funnel.

TIP: Kaffir lime leaves can be found in the fresh herbs section of your grocery store or at an Asian supermarket; they look like fresh bay leaves.

LEMONGRASS FIZZ

MAKES 1 DRINK

"This is the most delightful and refreshing version of a Fizz," says Mcson Salicetti, bartender at the Black Ant in New York City. "Made with rum and lemongrass, the Lemongrass Fizz combines delicious notes of citrus, sour, and bitter."

New to the United States is yuzu juice, which comes from a citrus fruit grown primarily in Japan. It has a complex, unique aroma, and its flavor can be described as a cross between grapefruit and tangerine, but with less tang. This makes it easy to add flavor to cocktails while maintaining balance.

PREP TIME: 5 MINUTES

FOR THE LEMONGRASS WATER

4 cups finely chopped lemongrass
2 cups water
Yuzu juice, to taste
1 ounce vodka

FOR THE COCKTAIL

1½ ounces light rum
¾ ounce freshly squeezed lime juice
½ ounce agave nectar
1 large egg white
1 dash Angostura bitters
1 dash Lemongrass Bitters (page 84)
1 lemongrass sprig, for garnish

TO MAKE THE LEMONGRASS WATER

1. Put the lemongrass in a blender.

2. With the machine running, slowly stream in the water until incorporated.

3. Strain through a cheesecloth into a bowl and discard the solids.

4. Add the yuzu juice and vodka.

5. Transfer to a container and refrigerate overnight.

1. In a shaker, combine 1 ounce of the lemongrass water with the rum, lime juice, agave nectar, and egg white.

2. Shake for 10 seconds, or until the egg white has turned foamy.

3. Fill the shaker two-thirds full with ice, and fill a coupe glass with ice water.

4. Shake for 10 to 15 seconds, or until chilled.

5. Discard the ice water, strain into the coupe glass, and add the Angostura and lemongrass bitters.

6. Serve garnished with the lemongrass sprig.

TIP: To prep lemongrass, peel away the tough outer leaves until the pale, tender center is revealed. Trim an inch from the top and bottom. Discard these parts along with the outer leaves. Then chop as called for in the recipe.

EAST INDIA COCKTAIL

MAKES 1 DRINK

This cocktail is a variation on a classic, the Sidecar, although you probably wouldn't guess that at first sip. The addition of pineapple juice to the usual trio of brandy, lemon juice, and Angostura takes things in a decidedly tropical direction, while the use of lemongrass bitters is a nod to the drink traditions of the region. There, lemongrass is brewed in hot water to make an herb tea.

PREP TIME: 5 MINUTES

1½ ounces brandy
½ ounce triple sec
1 ounce pineapple juice
½ ounce freshly squeezed
    lemon juice

2 dashes Angostura bitters
2 dashes Lemongrass
    Bitters (page 84)

1. Fill a shaker two-thirds full with ice, and fill a rocks glass with ice water.

2. In the shaker, combine the brandy, triple sec, pineapple juice, lemon juice, Angostura bitters, and lemongrass bitters.

3. Shake for 10 to 15 seconds, or until chilled.

4. Discard the ice water and strain into the rocks glass.

TIP: Take this cocktail to the next level by using fresh pineapple purée from a ripe pineapple. A ripe pineapple should smell very fruity and have a golden color on the outside.

LAVENDER BITTERS

MAKES 10 OUNCES

Edible flowers are all the rage in trendy restaurants, so why not bring a floral element to cocktails? The lavender bloom signals a shift toward warmer weather and, with it, lighter and brighter libations. Try these lavender bitters in refreshing gin-based drinks to give them an interesting twist.

PREP TIME: 1 MINUTE   INFUSING TIME: 3½ WEEKS

½ cup fresh edible lavender (preferably organic) or 4 teaspoons dried edible lavender (preferably organic)
Zest of 1 lemon
½ teaspoon orris root
1 cup high-proof vodka or grain alcohol
½ cup water
1 tablespoon honey

1. In a clean, clear glass jar with a tight-fitting lid, combine the lavender, lemon zest, orris root, and vodka, and seal with the lid. Make sure that the agents are completely submerged in the liquid.

2. Shake to combine and place in a well-trafficked area away from direct sunlight.

3. For 2 weeks, agitate the jar daily.

4. Place a snug-fitting funnel over another clean, clear glass jar. Line it with cheesecloth and strain the mixture, reserving the agents. Seal with the lid and place away from direct sunlight.

5. Transfer the agents to a saucepan and cover with the water.

6. Bring to a boil, then reduce to a simmer and cover with a lid; cook for 10 minutes.

7. Remove from the heat, let cool to room temperature, transfer to another clean, clear glass jar, and seal with the lid. >>

8. Shake to combine and place in a well-trafficked area away from direct sunlight.

9. For 1 week, agitate the jar daily.

10. Place a snug-fitting funnel over another clean, clear glass jar. Line it with cheesecloth and strain the liquid, discarding the agents.

11. Add this liquid and the honey to the vodka solution and shake to combine.

12. Wait 3 days before using, or until any floaters come to the top.

13. Place a snug-fitting funnel over another clean, clear glass jar. Line it with cheesecloth and strain the mixture, discarding any floaters.

14. Transfer to smaller, dark-colored bottles using a funnel.

TIP: Purchase fresh edible lavender, preferably organic, at the farmers' market, where you can ask questions about the product to make sure it is safe for cooking. Avoid purchasing lavender plants at garden centers, where the plants may have been treated with pesticides.

LAVENDER GIMLET

A gimlet is a simple cocktail every bartender should know: gin or vodka with a touch of lime cordial. Alex Valencia, mixologist at La Contenta in New York City, gives it an interesting spring twist with a good dose of lavender bitters. The distinctive floral element pairs nicely with gin.

PREP TIME: 10 MINUTES

2 ounces gin or vodka
¾ ounce freshly squeezed lime juice
¾ ounce Simple Syrup (page 107)

3 dashes Lavender Bitters (page 89), or Bar Keep Organic Lavender Bitters
1 strip lemon zest or 1 lavender sprig, for garnish

1. Fill a shaker two-thirds full with ice, and fill a martini glass with ice water.

2. In the shaker, combine the gin, lime juice, syrup, and bitters.

3. Shake for 10 to 15 seconds, or until chilled.

4. Discard the ice water, strain into the martini glass, and serve garnished with the lemon zest.

BLUEBERRY-LAVENDER HARD LEMONADE

MAKES 1 DRINK

This recipe comes from Malia Nahele, head bartender at Sansei Seafood Restaurant & Sushi Bar in Waikoloa, Hawaii. It's a breezy sipper perfect for a warm spring day. Pick up a book, find your favorite lawn chair, and watch the birds fly through the trees.

PREP TIME: 5 MINUTES

4 blueberries
4 ounces lemonade
1¼ ounces blueberry vodka, such as Hangar 1 Maine Wild Blueberry
1¼ ounces limoncello

3 dashes Lavender Bitters (page 89), or Bar Keep Organic Lavender Bitters
½ ounce sparkling water
1 lemon wheel, for garnish
1 mint sprig, for garnish

1. Place the blueberries in a Collins glass.

2. Using the flat end of a muddler, mash until the juice is extracted.

3. Fill the glass half full with ice, and then add the lemonade, vodka, limoncello, bitters, and sparkling water.

4. Stir for 30 seconds, or until well chilled.

5. Serve garnished with the lemon wheel and mint.

SORREL BITTERS

MAKES 10 OUNCES

Sorrel is one of spring's underappreciated treasures. Its lemony, tart flavor is too intense for salads, but it works beautifully in cocktails. Perk up any refreshing drink based on white spirits, such as gin, tequila blanco, or light rum, with a dose of these sorrel bitters.

PREP TIME: 1 MINUTE   INFUSING TIME: 3½ WEEKS

¼ cup sorrel leaves, torn
¼ cup chopped cucumber peel
2 tablespoons coriander seeds
Zest of ½ orange

½ ounce gentian root
1 cup high-proof light rum
½ cup water
1 tablespoon Rich Syrup (page 51)

1. In a clean, clear glass jar with a tight-fitting lid, combine the sorrel, cucumber peel, coriander seeds, orange zest, gentian root, and rum and seal with the lid. Make sure that the agents are completely submerged in the liquid.

2. Shake to combine and place in a well-trafficked area away from direct sunlight.

3. For 2 weeks, agitate the jar daily.

4. Place a snug-fitting funnel over another clean, clear glass jar. Line it with cheesecloth and strain the mixture, reserving the agents. Seal with the lid and place away from direct sunlight.

5. Transfer the agents to a saucepan and cover with the water.

6. Bring to a boil, then reduce to a simmer and cover with a lid; cook for 10 minutes.

7. Remove from the heat, let cool to room temperature, transfer to another clean, clear glass jar, and seal with the lid. >>

8. Shake to combine and place in a well-trafficked area away from direct sunlight.

9. For 1 week, agitate the jar daily.

10. Place a snug-fitting funnel over another clean, clear glass jar. Line it with cheesecloth and strain the liquid, discarding the agents.

11. Add this liquid and the syrup to the rum solution and shake to combine.

12. Wait 3 days before using, or until any floaters come to the top.

13. Place a snug-fitting funnel over another clean, clear glass jar. Line it with cheesecloth and strain the mixture, discarding any floaters.

14. Transfer to smaller, dark-colored bottles using a funnel.

STRAWBERRY-SORREL MOJITO

MAKES 1 DRINK

Fresh ingredients are the key to a good mojito, so seek out the best-looking lime, mint, and strawberries you can find for this cocktail.

Sorrel is an herb with a surprisingly strong citrus flavor, so a little goes a long way. Here, it acts as a bridge between the brightness of the lime and the sweetness of the strawberries.

PREP TIME: 5 MINUTES

1 lime, quartered
15 mint leaves
1 tablespoon powdered sugar
½ cup chopped strawberries

2 ounces light rum, such as
    Brugal Especial Extra Dry
3 dashes Sorrel Bitters (page 93)
2 ounces sparkling water
1 mint sprig, for garnish

1. In a mixing glass, combine the lime, mint leaves, and sugar.

2. Using the flat end of a muddler, mash the ingredients until the sugar dissolves completely.

3. Add the strawberries and mash until the juice is extracted.

4. Fill two-thirds full with ice and add the rum and bitters.

5. Stir for 10 to 15 seconds, or until well chilled.

6. Fill a Collins glass with crushed ice and strain the cocktail into the glass.

7. Top with the sparkling water and garnish with the mint.

SORREL DAIQUIRI

MAKES 1 DRINK

The daiquiri has many variations, but they all have one thing in common: Light rum is the spirit of choice, owing to its tropical origins. It might seem as though every fruit under the sun has been the subject of this drink, but there's one variation you probably haven't tried yet: a sorrel daiquiri. In the Caribbean, sorrel is a key ingredient in a refreshing summer cooler, and it is the inspiration behind this version of the drink.

PREP TIME: 5 MINUTES

FOR THE SORREL SYRUP

1½ ounces sorrel leaves, torn
1 cup sugar
1 cup water

FOR THE COCKTAIL

1½ ounces light rum, such as
    Brugal Especial Extra Dry
1 ounce freshly squeezed lime juice
3 dashes Sorrel Bitters (page 93)

TO MAKE THE SORREL SYRUP

1. In a medium saucepan, combine the sorrel, sugar, and water, and bring to a simmer over medium heat.

2. Maintain the simmer until the sugar is dissolved.

3. Let cool to room temperature and transfer to a container.

TO MAKE THE COCKTAIL

1. Fill a shaker two-thirds full with ice, and fill a rocks glass half full with ice.

2. Add the rum, lime juice, ½ ounce of the syrup, and the bitters to the shaker.

3. Shake for 10 to 15 seconds, or until chilled.

4. Strain into the rocks glass.

TIP: When making the syrup, avoid stirring the solution, which can cause crystals to form along the sides of the pan and burn.

CELERY BITTERS

MAKES 6 OUNCES

Celery is a vegetable that doesn't get a whole lot of attention, ordinarily—it's something that just blends into the background. But it can play a very noticeable role in savory cocktails. Celery does have a flavor—saline yet vegetal, like green beans—and giving it an extended soak in high-proof spirits brings that flavor front and center.

Create the tinctures required for this recipe using the procedure outlined in chapter 2 (see sidebar, "Your Tincture Primer," page 44).

PREP TIME: 1 MINUTE   INFUSING TIME: 29 DAYS

2½ ounces celery tincture
½ ounce gentian root tincture
½ ounce horehound tincture

½ ounce fennel seed tincture
2 ounces water

1. In a clean bowl, combine the celery, gentian root, horehound, and fennel seed tinctures, and mix thoroughly.

2. Add the water and, using a funnel, transfer to dark-colored bottles.

TIP: For a more intense celery flavor, try including some chopped celery leaves (as long as they look fresh) in the celery tincture.

SESAME HIGHBALL

MAKES 1 DRINK

Love savory drinks but looking for a change from the usual Bloody Mary? Cyllan Hicks, head bartender at New York City's Louie and Chan, has a wonderful cocktail for you to try. The rich flavor of toasted sesame gives this unusual, delicious highball a distinctive Asian-inspired flair.

PREP TIME: 1 MINUTE

2 ounces gin, such as Spring 44
⅛ teaspoon toasted sesame oil
¾ ounce freshly squeezed
   lemon juice
¾ ounce Simple Syrup (page 107)

Pinch salt
1½ ounces sparkling water
1 dash Celery Bitters (page 97)
1 cucumber wheel, for garnish

1. Fill a highball glass half full with ice.

2. In the following order, add the gin, sesame oil, lemon juice, syrup, salt, sparkling water, and bitters.

3. Using a bar spoon, stir a few times, and serve garnished with the cucumber wheel.

BLOODY MARY

Love it or hate it—no cocktail book would be complete without a recipe for a Bloody Mary. Celery bitters bring a crisp, refreshing element to balance the usual savory flavors of tomato and Worcestershire sauce in this version of the cocktail.

Interestingly, the origin of this American brunch classic is French. The drink was actually conceived in Paris at Harry's New York Bar during Prohibition, and imported here when it ended.

PREP TIME: 5 MINUTES

2 ounces vodka
2 ounces tomato juice
1 ounce freshly squeezed
   lemon juice

2 dashes Worcestershire sauce
3 dashes Celery Bitters (page 97)
¼ teaspoon kosher salt
1 celery stalk, for garnish

1. Fill a shaker two-thirds full with ice, and fill a highball glass with ice water.

2. Add the vodka, tomato juice, lemon juice, Worcestershire sauce, bitters, and salt to the shaker.

3. Shake for 10 to 15 seconds, or until chilled.

4. Discard the ice water, strain into the highball glass, and serve garnished with the celery stalk.

TIP: Puréeing fresh, ripe tomatoes instead of using store-bought juice makes a huge difference in this drink. Make sure to strain out the seeds before using.

STRAWBERRY BITTERS

MAKES 6¼ OUNCES

The appearance of strawberries is one of the most exciting things about spring produce. The first berries of the season are bursting with flavor, just waiting to be transformed into all kinds of exciting things—jams, pies, and, yes, cocktail ingredients. You might want to make a double batch of these bitters, as you're bound to find all kinds of ways to use them.

Create the tinctures required for this recipe using the procedure outlined in chapter 2 (see sidebar, "Your Tincture Primer," page 44).

PREP TIME: 1 MINUTE   INFUSING TIME: 29 DAYS

2½ ounces strawberry tincture
½ ounce horehound tincture
½ ounce lemon tincture
¼ ounce gentian root tincture

¼ ounce mint tincture
2 ounces water
¼ ounce Rich Syrup (page 51)

1. In a clean bowl, combine the strawberry, horehound, lemon, gentian root, and mint tinctures and mix thoroughly.

2. Add the water and syrup and, using a funnel, transfer to dark-colored bottles.

TIP: When shopping for fresh strawberries, pick through them to make sure they are free from fungus.

CLASSIC STRAWBERRY COLLINS

MAKES 1 DRINK

The Juniper Bar, which is a stone's throw from New York's Madison Square Garden, serves seasonal twists on classic cocktails. This take on the Tom Collins makes use of fresh strawberry purée, celebrating the bounty of spring. The addition of strawberry bitters accentuates the fruit's natural flavor.

PREP TIME: 1 MINUTE

1½ ounces London dry gin, such as Bombay Sapphire
¼ ounce freshly squeezed lemon juice

1 ounce fresh strawberry purée
3 dashes Strawberry Bitters (page 100)
2 ounces tonic water

1. Fill a shaker two-thirds full with ice, and fill a Collins glass half full with ice.

2. Add the gin, lemon juice, strawberry purée, and bitters to the shaker.

3. Shake for 10 to 15 seconds, or until chilled.

4. Strain into the Collins glass, top with the tonic water, and serve immediately.

TIP: No cocktail recipe is set in stone. Alcohol levels and flavor characteristics vary by bottling, so depending on what brand you use, you may wish to alter the proportions of a recipe to suit your taste.

AN EARLY SPRING STROLL

MAKES 1 DRINK AND 30 PICKLED STRAWBERRIES

Stephen Thomas of Restaurant Latour at Crystal Springs, located in Hamburg, New Jersey, concocted this imaginative cocktail in anticipation of the arrival of the first spring strawberries. In the restaurant, he uses Dutch's Spirits Colonial Cocktail Bitters to give the drink a complex, spicy, and floral element. However, a few dashes of homemade strawberry bitters also work beautifully in this cocktail.

PREP TIME: 5 MINUTES, PLUS OVERNIGHT
TO MAKE THE PICKLED STRAWBERRIES

FOR THE PICKLED GREEN STRAWBERRIES

1 bottle Champagne vinegar
½ cup sugar
10 peppercorns
2 bay leaves
2 tablespoons Maldon sea salt
3 quarts water
30 green strawberries

FOR THE COCKTAIL

2 kaffir lime leaves
1 sugar cube
5 dashes Strawberry Bitters (page 100) or Dutch's Spirits Colonial Cocktail Bitters
2 ounces moonshine, such as Dutch's Spirits Sugar Wash Moonshine
1½ ounces sparkling rosé, such as Jordan "J"

TO MAKE THE PICKLED GREEN STRAWBERRIES

1. In a large container, stir together the vinegar, sugar, peppercorns, bay leaves, salt, and water until the sugar and salt dissolve.

2. Add the strawberries, cover with a lid, and transfer to the refrigerator. The strawberries will keep for up to 6 months.

TO MAKE THE COCKTAIL

1. Fill a coupe glass with ice water.

2. In a mixing glass, combine 1 pickled strawberry with the kaffir lime leaves, sugar cube, and bitters.

3. Using the flat end of a muddler, mash the ingredients until the sugar dissolves completely.

4. Fill the glass half full with ice, and then add the moonshine.

5. Stir for 30 seconds, or until well chilled.

6. Discard the ice water, strain into the coupe glass, top with the sparkling rosé, and serve immediately.

THYME BITTERS

MAKES 6¼ OUNCES

Thyme may seem like an unusual choice for a bitters ingredient. After all, it is commonly used in a savory context to enhance the flavors of roast chicken, grilled whole fish, and herb-crusted lamb. But it also happens to work well in cocktails, complementing anything citrus-based.

Create the tinctures required for this recipe using the procedure outlined in chapter 2 (see sidebar, "Your Tincture Primer," page 44).

PREP TIME: 1 MINUTE   INFUSING TIME: 29 DAYS

2½ ounces thyme tincture
1 ounce lemon tincture
½ ounce cinchona bark tincture

2 ounces water
¼ ounce Rich Syrup (page 51)

1. In a clean bowl, combine the thyme, lemon, and cinchona bark tinctures and mix thoroughly.

2. Add the water and syrup and, using a funnel, transfer to dark-colored bottles.

THYME FOR A TOM COLLINS

MAKES 1 DRINK

The Tom Collins is beautiful in its simplicity, and that's one reason it's a classic. It's also the reason that it's hard to think of ways to improve on it. Modifying a classic should be done with restraint, and the addition of thyme bitters ushers in a bit of spring without going over the top.

PREP TIME: 1 MINUTE

2 ounces gin
1 ounce freshly squeezed
   lemon juice
1 ounce Simple Syrup (page 107)

3 dashes Thyme Bitters (page 104)
1 ounce club soda
1 maraschino cherry, for garnish
½ orange wheel, for garnish

1. Fill a shaker two-thirds full with ice, and fill a Collins glass half full with ice.

2. Add the gin, lemon juice, syrup, and bitters to the shaker.

3. Shake for 10 to 15 seconds, or until chilled.

4. Strain into the Collins glass, add the club soda, and serve garnished with the cherry and orange wheel.

WHAT THYME IS IT?

MAKES 1 DRINK

It's time for one of these cocktails. Find a comfortable spot on the porch or in the backyard, sit back, relax, and sip on this all afternoon long. The rays of sunshine never felt so good.

PREP TIME: 5 MINUTES

2 ounces gin
½ ounce triple sec
½ ounce freshly squeezed lime juice

2 dashes Angostura bitters
3 dashes Thyme Bitters (page 104)
1 thyme sprig, for garnish

1. Fill a shaker two-thirds full with ice, and fill a martini glass with ice water.

2. Add the gin, triple sec, lime juice, Angostura bitters, and thyme bitters to the shaker.

3. Shake for 10 to 15 seconds, or until chilled.

4. Discard the ice water, strain into the martini glass, and serve garnished with the thyme sprig.

Simple Syrup

MAKES 1½ CUPS

1 cup sugar
1 cup water

1. In a medium saucepan, combine the sugar and water and bring to a simmer over medium heat.

2. Stir gently until the sugar is dissolved.

3. Let cool to room temperature, and transfer to an airtight container. Simple syrup will keep in the refrigerator for up to 1 month.

Take It to the Next Level

Now that you've had a chance to sample spring's bounty in some interesting bitters, it's time to leave the nest and create your own custom bitters. Spring is all about lush green produce, so think about how to use fresh herbs to enhance your cocktails. Use these ideas to inspire your own bitters, cocktails, and pairings.

BITTERING AGENTS. Gentian root is the ideal choice for herb-based bitters, but horehound would be a fine substitute.

GREEN WITH ENVY. You've probably cooked with these herbs before but might not have used them in the context of cocktails.

- BASIL. Basil comes in many varieties, including lemon, holy, purple, and sweet. Sweet basil, or your garden-variety basil, has a mild peppery flavor. For an interesting twist, use basil bitters in cocktails where you would normally use mint bitters.

- CHIVES. Their crisp allium flavor is a hallmark of spring produce. Use in savory cocktails, such as the dirty martini or the Bloody Mary.

- OREGANO. In many people's minds, oregano is most closely associated with pizza. It's what turns marinara sauce meant for pasta into sauce meant for pizza, if you will. So what business does it have in a cocktail? Well, if you enjoyed using Thyme Bitters (page 104) in gin-based citrusy drinks, you might also like oregano bitters, which bring a similar savory element.

- TARRAGON. Its pronounced licorice flavor makes it a natural choice for citrusy drinks, as well as cocktails containing anise-flavored liqueurs, such as Herbsaint.

- WATERCRESS. Spicy watercress brings a horseradish-style heat to cocktails. Use watercress bitters to liven up savory cocktails.

TIME TO PLAY. Okay, now it's time for a homework assignment. Here are some cocktails you might want to try, along with their key components and suggested bitters. Take plenty of notes on what you like and don't like, so you can figure out what combinations work for you.

- ABBEY COCKTAIL. Gin, orange juice, oregano bitters.

- BLOODY CAESAR. Vodka, clam juice, chive bitters.

- CORPSE REVIVER. Gin, triple sec, Lillet, lemon juice, tarragon bitters.

- MICHELADA. Mexican beer, Clamato, chili powder, watercress bitters.

- STRAWBERRY-BASIL DAIQUIRI. Light rum, lime, fresh strawberries, basil bitters.

Stone fruit, fresh herbs, melons, and tomatoes line produce stands as far as the eye can see. Everything smells so fresh, so immediate, so vibrant, it's hard not to take the whole market home with you. Summer is an exciting time for produce.

CHAPTER FIVE
SUMMER

PEACH BITTERS

MAKES 10 OUNCES

Peaches are a true summertime treat. Nothing can compare to the flavor and aroma of a ripe peach at the height of summer. Here, vanilla bean and cinnamon complement the flavor of ripe yellow peaches.

PREP TIME: 1 MINUTE   INFUSING TIME: 3½ WEEKS

½ cup chopped ripe yellow peach
1 vanilla bean, split
1 cinnamon stick

½ teaspoon horehound
1 cup high-proof bourbon
½ cup water

1. In a clean, clear glass jar with a tight-fitting lid, combine the peach, vanilla bean, cinnamon stick, horehound, and bourbon and seal with the lid. Make sure that the agents are completely submerged in the liquid.

2. Shake to combine and place in a well-trafficked area away from direct sunlight.

3. For 2 weeks, agitate the jar daily.

4. Place a snug-fitting funnel over another clean, clear glass jar. Line it with cheesecloth and strain the mixture, reserving the agents. Seal with the lid and place away from direct sunlight.

5. Transfer the agents to a saucepan and cover with the water.

6. Bring to a boil, then reduce to a simmer and cover with a lid; cook for 10 minutes.

7. Remove from the heat, let cool to room temperature, transfer to another clean, clear glass jar, and seal with the lid.

8. Shake to combine and place in a well-trafficked area away from direct sunlight.

9. For 1 week, agitate the jar daily.

10. Place a snug-fitting funnel over another clean, clear glass jar. Line it with cheesecloth and strain the liquid, discarding the agents.

11. Add this liquid to the bourbon solution and shake to combine.

12. Wait 3 days before using, or until any floaters come to the top.

13. Place a snug-fitting funnel over another clean, clear glass jar. Line it with cheesecloth and strain the mixture, discarding any floaters.

14. Transfer to smaller, dark-colored bottles using a funnel.

TIP: If you decide to use white peaches, you may wish to substitute orris root for the horehound and ¼ cup chopped mint for the cinnamon to better match the fruit's floral notes.

BELLINI

Bellinis are served throughout the year, in defiance of the seasons. But wait until summer, when peaches overtake farmers' markets, and you'll be rewarded with a fantastic cocktail. Sometimes in life, the simple things really are the best.

PREP TIME: 1 MINUTE

1 ounce ripe white peach purée
4 ounces Prosecco

1 dash Peach Bitters (page 112)

1. Add the peach purée to a chilled Champagne flute, followed by the Prosecco and bitters.

2. Using a bar spoon, stir a few times, and serve.

TIP: If you're using a dropper to apply bitters, every 4 or 5 drops equals a dash.

PEACHY KEEN

MAKES 1 DRINK

Ripe peaches are essential to this summery cocktail. Unless they're ripe, you won't be able to get all the juices out of the fruit. They may seem to take an eternity to ripen, but the wait is worthwhile.

PREP TIME: 5 MINUTES

½ cup chopped ripe peach
5 mint leaves
1½ ounces bourbon

3 dashes Peach Bitters (page 112)
2 dashes Angostura bitters

1. In a rocks glass, combine the peach and mint leaves.

2. Using the flat end of a muddler, mash the ingredients until the juice is extracted.

3. Fill the glass half full with ice, and then add the bourbon, peach bitters, and Angostura bitters.

4. Stir for 30 seconds, or until well chilled.

TIP: To speed the ripening process, place peaches in a brown paper bag and seal the top. They should be ready in a few days.

CHERRY BITTERS

MAKES 10 OUNCES

Cherries are a fleeting treat. If you're lucky enough to have fresh, local cherries where you live, take advantage of the opportunity. In some regions, the season lasts only one month.

PREP TIME: 1 MINUTE   INFUSING TIME: 3¼ WEEKS

½ cup pitted cherries
1 vanilla bean, split
½ teaspoon wild cherry bark

1 cup high-proof bourbon
½ cup water

1. In a clean, clear glass jar with a tight-fitting lid, combine the pitted cherries, vanilla bean, wild cherry bark, and bourbon and seal with the lid. Make sure that the agents are completely submerged in the liquid.

2. Shake to combine and place in a well-trafficked area away from direct sunlight.

3. For 2 weeks, agitate the jar daily.

4. Place a snug-fitting funnel over another clean, clear glass jar. Line it with cheesecloth and strain the mixture, reserving the agents. Seal with the lid and place away from direct sunlight.

5. Transfer the agents to a saucepan and cover with the water.

6. Bring to a boil, then reduce to a simmer and cover with a lid; cook for 10 minutes.

7. Remove from the heat, let cool to room temperature, transfer to another clean, clear glass jar, and seal with the lid.

8. Shake to combine and place in a well-trafficked area away from direct sunlight.

9. For 1 week, agitate the jar daily.

10. Place a snug-fitting funnel over another clean, clear glass jar. Line it with cheesecloth and strain the liquid, discarding the agents.

11. Add this liquid to the bourbon solution and shake to combine.

12. Wait 3 days before using, or until any floaters come to the top.

13. Place a snug-fitting funnel over another clean, clear glass jar. Line it with cheesecloth and strain the mixture, discarding any floaters.

14. Transfer to smaller, dark-colored bottles using a funnel.

TIP: Although buying packaged bags of fresh cherries is definitely convenient, it's a good idea to pick through them when you get home to sort out the bad ones. Or, better yet, buy them loose at the store so you can choose the freshest ones.

AVIATION

Take flight with this cocktail, a refreshing combination of gin, lemon juice, and a touch of maraschino liqueur for sweetness and cherry flavor.

Some older recipes call for crème de violette, which gives this drink a distinctive purple hue and a floral element. It's not an essential ingredient, but it is worth exploring if you'd like to experiment a bit.

PREP TIME: 5 MINUTES

2½ ounces gin
¼ ounce maraschino liqueur

½ ounce freshly squeezed
lemon juice
3 dashes Cherry Bitters (page 116)

1. Fill a shaker two-thirds full with ice, and fill a martini glass with ice water.

2. Add the gin, maraschino liqueur, lemon juice, and bitters to the shaker.

3. Shake for 10 to 15 seconds, or until chilled.

4. Discard the ice water, strain into the martini glass, and serve immediately.

CHERRY GIN RICKEY

MAKES 1 DRINK

As originally conceived, the Gin Rickey was a very dry cocktail. This version has been updated for modern tastes with a touch of simple syrup. Cherry bitters are incorporated into the cocktail in homage to the soda fountain favorite, the cherry lime rickey.

PREP TIME: 1 MINUTE

¾ ounce freshly squeezed lime juice
¼ ounce Simple Syrup (page 107)
2½ ounces gin

1½ ounces sparkling water
3 dashes Cherry Bitters (page 116)
1 maraschino cherry, for garnish

1. Fill a Collins glass half full with ice.

2. In the following order, add the lime juice, syrup, gin, sparkling water, and bitters.

3. Using a bar spoon, stir a few times and serve garnished with the maraschino cherry.

RASPBERRY BITTERS

MAKES 10 OUNCES

Raspberries, mint, and lime are a revelatory combination. Use these bitters with summery drinks based on light rum, gin, or tequila blanco. For an interesting twist, you can also try using black or golden raspberries.

PREP TIME: 1 MINUTE   INFUSING TIME: 3¼ WEEKS

½ cup raspberries
¼ cup mint leaves
Zest of 1 lime
½ teaspoon horehound

1 cup high-proof vodka
  or grain alcohol
½ cup water
1 tablespoon Rich Syrup (page 51)

1. In a clean, clear glass jar with a tight-fitting lid, combine the raspberries, mint leaves, lime zest, horehound, and vodka and seal with the lid. Make sure that the agents are completely submerged in the liquid.

2. Shake to combine and place in a well-trafficked area away from direct sunlight.

3. For 2 weeks, agitate the jar daily.

4. Place a snug-fitting funnel over another clean, clear glass jar. Line it with cheesecloth and strain the mixture, reserving the agents. Seal with the lid and place away from direct sunlight.

5. Transfer the agents to a saucepan and cover with the water.

6. Bring to a boil, then reduce to a simmer and cover with a lid; cook for 10 minutes.

7. Remove from the heat, let cool to room temperature, transfer to another clean, clear glass jar, and seal with the lid.

8. Shake to combine and place in a well-trafficked area away from direct sunlight.

9. For 1 week, agitate the jar daily.

10. Place a snug-fitting funnel over another clean, clear glass jar. Line it with cheesecloth and strain the liquid, discarding the agents.

11. Add this liquid and the syrup to the vodka solution and shake to combine.

12. Wait 3 days before using, or until any floaters come to the top.

13. Place a snug-fitting funnel over another clean, clear glass jar. Line it with cheesecloth and strain the mixture, discarding any floaters.

14. Transfer to smaller, dark-colored bottles using a funnel.

EL FLORIDITA NO. 1

This cocktail is named after a bar in Cuba that Ernest Hemingway frequented. This drink was one of his favorites. The original version doesn't call for bitters, but raspberry bitters pair especially well with lime, and make for a nice addition to the drink.

PREP TIME: 5 MINUTES

2 ounces light rum, such as
　Brugal Especial Extra Dry
1 ounce freshly squeezed lime juice
½ ounce maraschino liqueur

½ ounce Simple Syrup (page 107)
3 dashes Raspberry
　Bitters (page 120)

1. Fill a shaker two-thirds full with ice, and fill a rocks glass with ice water.

2. Add the rum, lime juice, maraschino liqueur, syrup, and bitters to the shaker.

3. Shake for 10 to 15 seconds, or until chilled.

4. Discard the ice water, strain into the rocks glass, and serve immediately.

BENNETT COCKTAIL

MAKES 1 DRINK

This cocktail is a survivor of the Prohibition era. As it was first written, the cocktail was very dry. Here, the recipe has been updated for modern tastes.

PREP TIME: 5 MINUTES

2½ ounces gin
1 ounce freshly squeezed lime juice
½ ounce Simple Syrup (page 107)

2 dashes Angostura bitters
3 dashes Raspberry
Bitters (page 120)

1. Fill a shaker two-thirds full with ice, and fill a rocks glass with ice water.

2. Add the gin, lime juice, syrup, Angostura bitters, and raspberry bitters to the shaker.

3. Shake for 10 to 15 seconds, or until chilled.

4. Discard the ice water, strain into the rocks glass, and serve immediately.

TIP: Rolling a lime on the counter before cutting it helps release more juice.

HABANERO BITTERS

MAKES 10 OUNCES

Like a bit of heat in your cocktails? Then try these habanero bitters. Their heat is tempered by mint, leaving just a hint at the end of each sip.

PREP TIME: 1 MINUTE   INFUSING TIME: 3½ WEEKS

¼ cup seeded, stemmed, and chopped habanero chiles
¼ cup mint leaves
Zest of 1 lime
¼ teaspoon horehound

¼ teaspoon cinchona bark
1 cup high-proof tequila
½ cup water
1 tablespoon agave nectar

1. In a clean, clear glass jar with a tight-fitting lid, combine the habanero chiles, mint leaves, lime zest, horehound, cinchona bark, and tequila and seal with the lid. Make sure that the agents are completely submerged in the liquid.

2. Shake to combine and place in a well-trafficked area away from direct sunlight.

3. For 2 weeks, agitate the jar daily.

4. Place a snug-fitting funnel over another clean, clear glass jar. Line it with cheesecloth and strain the mixture, reserving the agents. Seal with the lid and place away from direct sunlight.

5. Transfer the agents to a saucepan and cover with the water.

6. Bring to a boil, then reduce to a simmer and cover with a lid; cook for 10 minutes.

7. Remove from the heat, let cool to room temperature, transfer to another clean, clear glass jar, and seal with the lid.

8. Shake to combine and place in a well-trafficked area away from direct sunlight.

9. For 1 week, agitate the jar daily.

10. Place a snug-fitting funnel over another clean, clear glass jar. Line it with cheesecloth and strain the liquid, discarding the agents.

11. Add this liquid and the agave nectar to the tequila solution and shake to combine.

12. Wait 3 days before using, or until any floaters come to the top.

13. Place a snug-fitting funnel over another clean, clear glass jar. Line it with cheesecloth and strain the mixture, discarding any floaters.

14. Transfer to smaller, dark-colored bottles using a funnel.

TIP: When working with hot peppers, wear gloves to protect your hands from the capsaicin, a compound that gives chiles their heat and causes a burning sensation on skin.

DIABLA DULCE

MAKES 1 DRINK

This diabolical creation is courtesy of Amy Fahland, restaurant manager at Sansei Seafood Restaurant & Sushi Bar in Kapalua, Hawaii. It packs a bit of heat thanks to the habanero bitters, but don't worry, it's not overpowering. In fact, the habanero blends in nicely with the tropical fruit flavors of the drink.

PREP TIME: 10 MINUTES

FOR THE HOMEMADE
SWEET-AND-SOUR

1 ounce freshly squeezed
orange juice
1 ounce freshly squeezed
lemon juice
1 ounce freshly squeezed lime juice
1 ounce Simple Syrup (page 107)

FOR THE COCKTAIL

1¼ ounces tequila, such
as Tres Agaves
¼ ounce green Chartreuse
⅛ ounce mezcal, such as Sombra
1 dash passion fruit purée
1 dash Habanero Bitters (page 124)
Black sea salt, for the rim
1 piece dried mango, for garnish

TO MAKE THE HOMEMADE SWEET-AND-SOUR

1. In a small bowl, stir together the orange juice, lemon juice, lime juice, and syrup until combined.

2. Cover and refrigerate until ready to use.

1. Fill a shaker two-thirds full with ice, and fill a martini glass with ice water.

2. Add the tequila, Chartreuse, mezcal, passion fruit purée, 1 ounce of the sweet-and-sour, and the bitters to the shaker. Shake for 10 to 15 seconds, or until chilled.

3. Discard the ice water, and coat half of the rim with black sea salt.

4. Strain into the martini glass and serve garnished with the dried mango.

TIP: You can find passion fruit purée online. Some good brands to try include First Call and Perfect Purée.

MEXICO LIBRE

MAKES 1 DRINK

This is a variation on the humble Cuba Libre, which is usually made with light rum. Habanero bitters add a fruity heat to the drink, which rounds out the sweetness of the cola. Serve this for a casual get-together with friends on the weekend.

PREP TIME: 1 MINUTE

2 ounces tequila blanco such as Roca Patrón Silver
½ ounce freshly squeezed lime juice
3 ounces cola

3 dashes Habanero Bitters (page 124)
1 lime wedge, for garnish

1. Fill a highball glass half full with ice.

2. In the following order, add the tequila, lime juice, cola, and bitters.

3. Using a bar spoon, stir a few times and serve garnished with the lime wedge.

CUCUMBER BITTERS

MAKES 6 OUNCES

On a hot summer day, the idea of enjoying the cool taste of a cucumber is just as welcoming as a brisk breeze over the water. And their slight astringency makes them an ideal candidate as a bitters ingredient. These cucumber bitters add a burst of freshness to your favorite summer cocktails that lingers on the palate.

Create the tinctures required for this recipe using the procedure outlined in chapter 2 (see sidebar, "Your Tincture Primer," page 44).

PREP TIME: 1 MINUTE   INFUSING TIME: 27 DAYS

2½ ounces cucumber tincture
½ ounce gentian root tincture
½ ounce mint tincture

½ ounce lime tincture
2 ounces water

1. In a clean bowl, combine the cucumber, gentian root, mint, and lime tinctures and mix thoroughly.

2. Add the water and, using a funnel, transfer to dark-colored bottles.

TIP: Use only the peel to make the cucumber tincture, and save the flesh for your favorite salad. Using the flesh would water down the flavor of the tincture.

MINT JULEP

MAKES 1 DRINK

Cool, pleasantly sweet, and refreshing—this is, quite possibly, the perfect summer cocktail. Take long, slow sips out on the porch, and enjoy the weather. Cucumber bitters are a nice addition to the drink, as they pair well with the mint.

PREP TIME: 1 MINUTE

½ ounce Simple Syrup (page 107)
15 mint leaves
3 dashes Cucumber
   Bitters (page 129)
3 dashes Angostura bitters

2 ounces bourbon
½ cup crushed ice, plus
   more as needed
1 mint sprig, for garnish

1. In a highball glass, combine the syrup, mint leaves, cucumber bitters, and Angostura bitters.

2. Using the flat end of a muddler, mash the ingredients until the mint leaves are bruised.

3. Add the bourbon and crushed ice and, using a bar spoon, stir for 20 seconds, or until frost forms on the glass.

4. Top with more crushed ice until it forms a slight bubble over the top of the glass, insert cocktail straws, and serve garnished with the mint sprig.

TIP: Juleps give you a chance to be creative. Although bourbon and simple syrup are the standard combination, there's no reason why you couldn't use another amber spirit, such as dark rum or brandy, as a base, or even substitute a fruit-flavored liqueur, such as maraschino, for the simple syrup.

PISCO SOUR

MAKES 1 DRINK

When ordering them at a restaurant, Pisco Sours can seem exotic, and perhaps difficult to make at home. But really, they're not any more difficult to make than any other shaken cocktail. The secret lies in the use of egg white, which gives the cocktail a smooth, foamy top.

PREP TIME: 5 MINUTES

2 ounces pisco brandy
½ ounce freshly squeezed
   lemon juice
½ ounce freshly squeezed lime juice
½ ounce Simple Syrup (page 107)

1 large egg white
2 dashes Angostura bitters
2 dashes Cucumber
   Bitters (page 129)

1. Fill a shaker two-thirds full with ice, and fill a coupe glass with ice water.

2. Add the pisco brandy, lemon juice, lime juice, syrup, and egg white to the shaker.

3. Shake for 10 to 15 seconds, or until chilled.

4. Discard the ice water, strain into the coupe glass, and add the Angostura and cucumber bitters on top.

TIP: Because this drink uses uncooked egg whites, use the freshest eggs possible. If you're worried about food-borne pathogens, buy pasteurized eggs.

COCONUT BITTERS

MAKES 6¼ OUNCES

On a hot summer day, have a sip of something nice and fruity. These coconut bitters are the perfect complement to tropically inspired drinks, which are a mainstay of the season.

Create the tinctures required for this recipe using the procedure outlined in chapter 2 (see sidebar, "Your Tincture Primer," page 44).

PREP TIME: 1 MINUTE   INFUSING TIME: 29 DAYS

3 ounces coconut tincture
½ ounce horehound tincture
½ ounce cardamom tincture

2 ounces water
¼ ounce Rich Syrup (page 51)

1. In a clean bowl, combine the coconut, horehound, and cardamom tinctures, and mix thoroughly.

2. Add the water and syrup and, using a funnel, transfer to dark-colored bottles.

TIP: Use large, unsweetened coconut flakes (rather than shredded coconut) to make the tincture for this recipe; they are easier to strain.

MADRAS MULE

MAKES 1 DRINK

This drink was inspired by the Moscow Mule. A simple concoction, it was invented by Jack Morgan, proprietor of the Cock 'n' Bull in Los Angeles. The Moscow Mule was credited with popularizing vodka in America. A touch of coconut bitters transforms this drink into a tropical sipper, perfect for whiling away the hours under the sun.

PREP TIME: 1 MINUTE

2 ounces vodka

2 ounces ginger beer

5 dashes Coconut Bitters (page 132)

1 lime wedge, for garnish

1. Fill a highball glass half full with ice.

2. In the following order, add the vodka, ginger beer, and bitters.

3. Using a bar spoon, stir a few times and serve garnished with the lime wedge.

MANGO MARGARITA

MAKES 1 DRINK

Get the party started with this fantastic margarita recipe from Juniper Bar, located in midtown Manhattan in New York. Mangoes—most of which come to the United States from Mexico—reach peak flavor in the summer. So what are you waiting for? The taste of paradise is calling.

PREP TIME: 5 MINUTES

1½ ounces tequila blanco such as Patrón Silver
½ ounce triple sec such as Cointreau
2 ounces mango purée

1½ ounces freshly squeezed lime juice
5 dashes Coconut Bitters (page 132)
1 lime wedge, for garnish

1. Fill a shaker two-thirds full with ice, and fill a margarita glass half full with ice.

2. Add the tequila, triple sec, mango purée, lime juice, and bitters to the shaker.

3. Shake for 10 to 15 seconds, or until chilled.

4. Strain into the margarita glass and serve garnished with the lime wedge.

TIP: Be sure to use ripe mangoes for this recipe. Ripe mangoes are tinged mostly with gold and red on the outside, have a few black spots, and smell strongly of tropical fruit.

MINT BITTERS

MAKES 6¼ OUNCES

Mint bitters are a wonderful choice for livening up your favorite summer cocktails. Mint's herbal, slightly sweet flavor makes it an ideal partner for a variety of fruits, including pineapple, peach, mango, and lime.

When shopping for mint, look for deep green leaves free from bruises, spots, or other blemishes.

Create the tinctures required for this recipe using the procedure outlined in chapter 2 (see sidebar, "Your Tincture Primer," page 44).

PREP TIME: 1 MINUTE   INFUSING TIME: 27 DAYS

2 ounces mint tincture
1 ounce orange tincture
½ ounce lemon tincture

½ ounce gentian root tincture
2 ounces water
¼ ounce Rich Syrup (page 51)

1. In a clean bowl, combine the mint, orange, lemon and gentian root tinctures, and mix thoroughly.

2. Add the water and syrup and, using a funnel, transfer to dark-colored bottles.

    TIP: To shorten the time required to make the mint tincture, slice the mint leaves into thin strips.

BLACK-EYED SUSAN

MAKES 1 DRINK

Colorful name aside, this is one delicious cocktail. Mint bitters round out the flavors in this drink and give it a nice summer flourish. This cocktail is a great way to get the party started, whether you're throwing a barbecue or a pool party.

PREP TIME: 1 MINUTE

1 ounce vodka
2 ounces golden rum such as
    Brugal Añejo
¼ ounce triple sec
2 ounces freshly squeezed
    orange juice

1 ounce pineapple juice
3 dashes Mint Bitters (page 135)
1 lime wedge (optional)
½ orange wheel, for garnish

1. Fill a Collins glass half full with crushed ice.

2. In the following order, add the vodka, rum, triple sec, orange juice, pineapple juice, and bitters.

3. Using a bar spoon, stir a few times, squeeze the lime wedge into the drink (if using), and drop it in.

4. Serve garnished with the orange wheel.

MAIDEN'S PRAYER

MAKES 1 DRINK

This is a version of a drink created by Harry Craddock, one of many bartenders who left the United States for Europe during Prohibition. During his time at the Savoy Hotel in London, he created many cocktails that modern mixologists turn to for inspiration today. Here, mint bitters complement the flavors of citrus nicely.

PREP TIME: 5 MINUTES

2½ ounces gin
½ ounce triple sec
½ ounce freshly squeezed
  lemon juice

½ ounce freshly squeezed
  orange juice
2 dashes Angostura bitters
3 dashes Mint Bitters (page 135)

1. Fill a shaker two-thirds full with ice, and fill a rocks glass with ice water.

2. Add the gin, triple sec, lemon juice, orange juice, Angostura bitters, and mint bitters to the shaker.

3. Shake for 10 to 15 seconds, or until chilled.

4. Discard the ice water, strain into the rocks glass, and serve immediately.

Take It to the Next Level

Summer is an exciting and challenging time for the bitters enthusiast. Why? Great ingredients appear in such abundance at markets that it can be challenging to stay focused. Not to worry, though: Keep reading for tips that will narrow down your list to the essentials and help you start thinking coherently about making your own bitters using summer ingredients. Here are some ideas for bitters, cocktails, and pairings that you can try as an exercise.

BITTERING AGENTS. Wild cherry bark is an excellent choice for dark stone fruit, such as plums and pluots (a hybrid of a plum and an apricot), while vegetal gentian root is fantastic for green herbs. Use cinchona bark to complement fruit that has a sweet-tart flavor, such as blackberries and mangoes. And when in doubt, default to horehound, which is a great all-rounder.

HEAD TO THE PRODUCE STAND. Here are some ingredients you'll definitely want to pick up next time you head out for groceries.

- APRICOTS. Their intense flavor is complemented well by vanilla bean as well as mint. Choose apricots that are fragrant and have a red blush. Use apricot bitters to liven up bourbon-based sippers.

- BLACKBERRIES. Blackberries and lime are a great combination. Use blackberry bitters to make variations on daiquiris and juleps.

- CILANTRO. Cilantro may seem like an unusual ingredient in a cocktail, but adding a dash or two of cilantro bitters to savory drinks is definitely worth trying.

- MANGOES. Punch up your rum punch with a dose of mango bitters. Choose mangoes that are pleasantly fragrant and have small black spots along the skin, indicating ripeness.

- **PLUMS.** Plums and pluots come in a diverse array of flavors and colors. Experiment to find out what works best. Tropical drinks are a good place to start.

- **TOMATOES.** Tomato bitters are fantastic in—what else?—Bloody Marys and Micheladas.

- **WATERMELON.** Did someone say margarita? Up your margarita game with a dash of watermelon bitters.

TIME TO PLAY. Okay, now it's time for a homework assignment. Here is a list of cocktails worth seeking out, along with their key components and suggested bitters. Take notes on what works for you and what doesn't; everyone's flavor preferences are personal.

- **APRICOT JULEP.** Ripe apricots, mint, bourbon, apricot bitters.

- **BACARDI COCKTAIL.** Light rum, lime juice, grenadine, blackberry bitters.

- **BLOODY MARY MARTINI.** Vodka, freshly squeezed tomato juice, tomato bitters.

- **RUM PUNCH.** Light rum, pineapple juice, orange juice, lime juice, grenadine, mango bitters.

- **WATERMELON MARGARITA.** Tequila blanco, triple sec, lime juice, watermelon purée, watermelon bitters.

With the days growing shorter and the leaves changing color, it's time to shift toward cocktails with warm, comforting flavors. Pair spices with amber spirits such as brandy, whiskey, Scotch, or rye, and create cocktails with uniquely fall ingredients such as apples, cranberries, or pomegranates.

CHAPTER SIX

FALL

ALLSPICE BITTERS

MAKES 10 OUNCES

Allspice berries give off a warm, sweet aroma and, incidentally, are the main ingredient in jerk seasoning. In the context of drinks, allspice is one of the spices often used to make mulled wine, a comforting fall favorite. Allspice can also be used in whiskey-based drinks or with other amber-hued spirits, and it complements the flavor of cranberries nicely.

PREP TIME: 10 MINUTES   INFUSING TIME: 3½ WEEKS

¼ cup allspice berries
Zest of 1 orange
1 (1-inch) piece ginger,
    peeled and julienned

½ teaspoon cinchona bark
1 cup high-proof bourbon
½ cup water
1 tablespoon Rich Syrup (page 51)

1. In a clean, clear glass jar with a tight-fitting lid, combine the allspice, orange zest, ginger, cinchona bark, and bourbon and seal with the lid. Make sure that the agents are completely submerged in the liquid.

2. Shake to combine and place in a well-trafficked area away from direct sunlight.

3. For 2 weeks, agitate the jar daily.

4. Place a snug-fitting funnel over another clean, clear glass jar. Line it with cheesecloth and strain the mixture, reserving the agents. Seal with the lid and place away from direct sunlight.

5. Transfer the agents to a saucepan and cover with the water.

6. Bring to a boil, then reduce to a simmer and cover with a lid; cook for 10 minutes.

7. Remove from the heat, let cool to room temperature, transfer to another clean, clear glass jar, and seal with the lid.

8. Shake to combine and place in a well-trafficked area away from direct sunlight.

9. For 1 week, agitate the jar daily.

10. Place a snug-fitting funnel over another clean, clear glass jar. Line it with cheesecloth and strain the liquid, discarding the agents.

11. Add this liquid and the syrup to the bourbon solution and shake to combine.

12. Wait 3 days before using, or until any floaters come to the top.

13. Place a snug-fitting funnel over another clean, clear glass jar. Line it with cheesecloth and strain the mixture, discarding any floaters.

14. Transfer to smaller, dark-colored bottles using a funnel.

FALL BACK

MAKES 1 DRINK

If the coming of fall has you longing for just a few more days of summer, this cocktail ought to help smooth the transition.

Brandy is an oft-overlooked spirit as a base for cocktails, but it has a wonderful flavor that marries well with warming spices, such as allspice. Triple sec brings a touch of citrusy sweetness to this cocktail, while dry vermouth keeps it in balance.

PREP TIME: 5 MINUTES

1½ ounces brandy
1½ ounces dry vermouth
½ ounce triple sec

3 dashes Allspice Bitters (page 142)
1 strip orange zest, for garnish

1. Fill a mixing glass two-thirds full with ice, and fill a martini glass with ice water.

2. Add the brandy, vermouth, triple sec, and bitters to the mixing glass.

3. Using a bar spoon, stir for 30 seconds, or until chilled.

4. Discard the ice water, strain into the martini glass, and serve garnished with the orange zest.

TIP: Generally, brandy is designated by one of three grades. They are, in ascending order: VS (very special), VSOP (very superior old pale), and XO (extra old). For mixing cocktails, VS will do very nicely.

CRANBERRY WHISKEY SOUR

MAKES 1 DRINK

Whiskey sours are easy to make, so there's no need to resort to that premade sour mix that has given this drink a bad rap. This elegant take on the bar classic features one of fall's most iconic ingredients: cranberries. A few dashes of allspice bitters give a pleasant sweetness on the nose, rounding out the tanginess of the drink.

PREP TIME: 5 MINUTES

2½ ounces bourbon
1 ounce freshly squeezed
   lemon juice

½ ounce cranberry juice cocktail
½ ounce Simple Syrup (page 107)
3 dashes Allspice Bitters (page 142)

1. Fill a shaker two-thirds full with ice, and fill a double rocks glass half full with ice.

2. Add the bourbon, lemon juice, cranberry juice cocktail, syrup, and bitters to the shaker.

3. Shake for 10 to 15 seconds, or until chilled.

4. Strain into the rocks glass and serve immediately.

TIP: As a rule of thumb, cocktails featuring fruit juice are shaken.

POMEGRANATE BITTERS

MAKES 10 OUNCES

When it comes to fall fruit, apples, cranberries, and pears bask in the limelight, but pomegranates deserve some attention, too. Their unique flavor pairs nicely with warm fall spices as well as cool mint. Introduce these bitters to any cocktail that features grenadine to give it an extra burst of pomegranate essence.

PREP TIME: 1 MINUTE   INFUSING TIME: 3½ WEEKS

½ cup pomegranate seeds
¼ cup mint leaves
Zest of 1 lemon
½ teaspoon horehound

1 cup high-proof vodka
  or grain alcohol
½ cup water
1 tablespoon Rich Syrup (page 51)

1. In a clean, clear glass jar with a tight-fitting lid, combine the pomegranate seeds, mint leaves, lemon zest, horehound, and vodka and seal with the lid. Make sure that the agents are completely submerged in the liquid.

2. Shake to combine and place in a well-trafficked area away from direct sunlight.

3. For 2 weeks, agitate the jar daily.

4. Place a snug-fitting funnel over another clean, clear glass jar. Line it with cheesecloth and strain the mixture, reserving the agents. Seal with the lid and place away from direct sunlight.

5. Transfer the agents to a saucepan and cover with the water.

6. Bring to a boil, then reduce to a simmer and cover with a lid; cook for 10 minutes.

7. Remove from the heat, let cool to room temperature, transfer to another clean, clear glass jar, and seal with the lid.

8. Shake to combine and place in a well-trafficked area away from direct sunlight.

9. For 1 week, agitate the jar daily.

10. Place a snug-fitting funnel over another clean, clear glass jar. Line it with cheesecloth and strain the liquid, discarding the agents.

11. Add this liquid and the syrup to the vodka solution, and shake to combine.

12. Wait 3 days before using, or until any floaters come to the top.

13. Place a snug-fitting funnel over another clean, clear glass jar. Line it with cheesecloth and strain the mixture, discarding any floaters.

14. Transfer to smaller, dark-colored bottles using a funnel.

TIP: Getting the seeds out of a pomegranate doesn't have to be hard work. In fact, it can be a lot of fun. Simply cut the fruit into wedges and hold each wedge, cut-side down, over a large bowl. Whack repeatedly with the back of a wooden spoon and the seeds will fall right out.

POMEGRANATE SIDECAR

MAKES 1 DRINK

How the Sidecar got its name is up for debate—one story, told by David Embury, author of *The Fine Art of Mixing Drinks*, is that an acquaintance of his used to accompany him in the sidecar of a motorcycle on the way to their usual watering hole in Paris. But one thing that is clear is that the Sidecar is the foundation for a number of drinks people hold dear today, such as the margarita.

This twist on the classic calls for a bit of grenadine to bring pomegranate flavor to the drink, and Grand Marnier, an orange-flavored Cognac, stands in for the usual triple sec to balance the overall flavor.

PREP TIME: 5 MINUTES

1½ ounces brandy
½ ounce Grand Marnier
½ ounce grenadine
1 ounce freshly squeezed
    lemon juice

2 dashes Pomegranate
    Bitters (page 146)
1 tablespoon pomegranate
    seeds, for garnish

1. Fill a shaker two-thirds full with ice, and fill a martini glass with ice water.

2. Add the brandy, Grand Marnier, grenadine, lemon juice, and bitters to the shaker.

3. Shake for 10 to 15 seconds, or until chilled.

4. Discard the ice water, strain into the martini glass, and serve garnished with the pomegranate seeds.

TIP: If you'd like a sweeter, lower-proof cocktail, substitute triple sec for the Grand Marnier.

APPLEJACK ROSÉ

MAKES 1 DRINK

Looking to step up your fall cocktail game? Here's a lovely seasonal cocktail from Stephen Thomas of Restaurant Latour at Crystal Springs, located in Hamburg, New Jersey. Instead of using grenadine, he makes his own pomegranate syrup to give the cocktail fresher, brighter flavors.

PREP TIME: 5 MINUTES

FOR THE POMEGRANATE SYRUP

12 ounces superfine sugar
12 ounces pomegranate
    juice, such as POM

FOR THE PEAR AND PEACH GRANITA

2 cups strained peach nectar
2 cups strained pear juice
2 cups Simple Syrup (page 107)

FOR THE COCKTAIL

2 ounces applejack, such as
    Black Dirt Distillery
5 dashes Pomegranate
    Bitters (page 146)

TO MAKE THE POMEGRANATE SYRUP

1. In a large bowl, stir the sugar and juice until the sugar dissolves.

2. Transfer to a container with a lid and store in the refrigerator.

TO MAKE THE PEAR AND PEACH GRANITA

1. In a shallow casserole, mix the peach nectar, pear juice, and syrup until well combined.

2. Place in the freezer for 2 hours, or until completely frozen.

TO MAKE THE COCKTAIL

1. Fill a shaker two-thirds full with ice, and fill a coupe glass with ice water.

2. Add the applejack, ¾ ounce of the pomegranate syrup, and the bitters to the shaker. >>

3. Shake for 10 to 15 seconds, or until chilled.

4. Discard the ice water and add ½ cup of the pear and peach granita to the coupe glass.

5. Strain the cocktail over the granita.

TIP: Using a fork, scrape the edges of the granita toward the center every 20 to 30 minutes while it is in the freezer to give it a nice texture.

CRANBERRY BITTERS

MAKES 10 OUNCES

If sweater season has arrived, it's probably time to look for fresh cranberries and make these fantastic cranberry bitters.

In the field of cranberry preparations—cranberry jam, cranberry salsa, cranberry sauce, pickled cranberries—cranberry bitters are a standout. Use these bitters for an autumnal twist on your favorite cool-weather cocktails.

PREP TIME: 10 MINUTES   INFUSING TIME: 3½ WEEKS

½ cup fresh cranberries, halved
1 cinnamon stick
Zest of 1 orange
Zest of 1 lemon
1 (1-inch) piece ginger,
   peeled and julienned

½ teaspoon cinchona bark
1 cup high-proof vodka
   or grain alcohol
½ cup water
1 tablespoon honey

1. In a clean, clear glass jar with a tight-fitting lid, combine the cranberries, cinnamon stick, orange zest, lemon zest, ginger, cinchona bark, and vodka and seal with the lid. Make sure that the agents are completely submerged in the liquid.

2. Shake to combine and place in a well-trafficked area away from direct sunlight.

3. For 2 weeks, agitate the jar daily.

4. Place a snug-fitting funnel over another clean, clear glass jar. Line it with cheesecloth and strain the mixture, reserving the agents. Seal with the lid and place away from direct sunlight.

5. Transfer the agents to a saucepan and cover with the water.

6. Bring to a boil, then reduce to a simmer and cover with a lid; cook for 10 minutes. >>

7. Remove from the heat, let cool to room temperature, transfer to another clean, clear glass jar, and seal with the lid.

8. Shake to combine and place in a well-trafficked area away from direct sunlight.

9. For 1 week, agitate the jar daily.

10. Place a snug-fitting funnel over another clean, clear glass jar. Line it with cheesecloth and strain the liquid, discarding the agents.

11. Add this liquid and the honey to the vodka solution and shake to combine.

12. Wait 3 days before using, or until any floaters come to the top.

13. Place a snug-fitting funnel over another clean, clear glass jar. Line it with cheesecloth and strain the mixture, discarding any floaters.

14. Transfer to smaller, dark-colored bottles using a funnel.

TIP: Fresh cranberries can be stored in the refrigerator for up to 2 months.

THE LAST BAY BREEZE

MAKES 1 DRINK

When the approach of fall is imminent, turn to this simple cocktail to give one last nod to summer. A splash of pineapple is a reminder of all the fun under the sun, and a touch of cranberry serves as a preview of the bounty of fall to come. So go ahead: Take a sip and enjoy the last warm breeze over the bay in the fading light of the sunset.

PREP TIME: 1 MINUTE

2½ ounces light rum such as
  Brugal Especial Extra Dry
1½ ounces cranberry juice cocktail
1 ounce pineapple juice

3 dashes Cranberry Bitters
  (page 151)
1 lime wedge, for garnish

1. Fill a highball glass half full with ice.

2. In the following order, add the rum, cranberry juice cocktail, pineapple juice, and bitters.

3. Using a bar spoon, stir a few times, and serve garnished with the lime wedge.

BRONX IN THE FALL

MAKES 1 DRINK

The New York Botanical Garden lies north of all the hustle and bustle of Manhattan, in a quiet section of the Bronx. Fall is a great time to visit and bear witness to the changing colors of the leaves. Such was the inspiration behind this twist on the classic Bronx cocktail, which, incidentally, was named after the zoo.

PREP TIME: 5 MINUTES

1½ ounces gin
½ ounce sweet vermouth
½ ounce dry vermouth
½ ounce freshly squeezed
  orange juice

1 ounce cranberry juice cocktail
3 dashes Cranberry Bitters
  (page 151)
1 strip orange zest, for garnish

1. Fill a shaker two-thirds full with ice, and fill a martini glass with ice water.

2. Add the gin, sweet vermouth, dry vermouth, orange juice, cranberry juice cocktail, and bitters to the shaker.

3. Shake for 10 to 15 seconds, or until chilled.

4. Discard the ice water, strain into the martini glass, and serve garnished with the orange zest.

SAFFRON BITTERS

MAKES 10 OUNCES

Lend a touch of the exotic to your cocktails with these vibrant red threads harvested from the crocus plant. Their flavor and aroma are incomparable—heady, savory, and rich. Just a drop or two of saffron bitters will imbue your drinks with a lovely red-orange hue.

PREP TIME: 1 MINUTE   INFUSING TIME: 3½ WEEKS

---

2 teaspoons saffron threads
3 cardamom pods, crushed
Zest of 1 orange
½ teaspoon orris root

1 cup high-proof vodka
  or grain alcohol
½ cup water
1 tablespoon Rich Syrup (page 51)

1. In a clean, clear glass jar with a tight-fitting lid, combine the saffron, cardamom, orange zest, orris root, and vodka and seal with the lid. Make sure that the agents are completely submerged in the liquid.

2. Shake to combine and place in a well-trafficked area away from direct sunlight.

3. For 2 weeks, agitate the jar daily.

4. Place a snug-fitting funnel over another clean, clear glass jar. Line it with cheesecloth and strain the mixture, reserving the agents. Seal with the lid and place away from direct sunlight.

5. Transfer the agents to a saucepan and cover with the water.

6. Bring to a boil, then reduce to a simmer and cover with a lid; cook for 10 minutes.

7. Remove from the heat, let cool to room temperature, transfer to another clean, clear glass jar, and seal with the lid. >>

8. Shake to combine and place in a well-trafficked area away from direct sunlight.

9. For 1 week, agitate the jar daily.

10. Place a snug-fitting funnel over another clean, clear glass jar. Line it with cheesecloth and strain the liquid, discarding the agents.

11. Add this liquid and the syrup to the vodka solution and shake to combine.

12. Wait 3 days before using, or until any floaters come to the top.

13. Place a snug-fitting funnel over another clean, clear glass jar. Line it with cheesecloth and strain the mixture, discarding any floaters.

14. Transfer to smaller, dark-colored bottles using a funnel.

TIP: When shopping for saffron, look for threads that are bright red and dry.

SAFFRON CHAMPAGNE COCKTAIL

MAKES 1 DRINK

This is probably one of the easiest cocktails you'll come across in the book. And it tastes absolutely decadent. Saffron bitters lend an exotic touch to a drink that is already luxurious in its own right.

PREP TIME: 1 MINUTE

1 sugar cube
4 dashes Saffron Bitters (page 155)

5 ounces Champagne
or sparkling wine

1. Place the sugar cube in a Champagne flute and soak with the bitters.

2. Top with the Champagne and serve immediately.

TIP: Do not attempt to freeze Champagne or sparkling wine. Doing so would cause the cork to pop out, or even cause the glass to shatter, leaving a mess in your freezer.

ALGONQUIN COCKTAIL

MAKES 1 DRINK

This is a recipe that was nearly lost to time. And if you try to look it up, you'll see evidence of that in just about every recipe you find. Hardly anyone can agree on what the true formula is for this cocktail, but that leaves plenty of room for creativity.

PREP TIME: 5 MINUTES

1½ ounces rye whiskey
½ ounce dry vermouth

1 ounce pineapple juice
3 dashes Saffron Bitters (page 155)

1. Fill a mixing glass two-thirds full with ice, and fill a martini glass with ice water.

2. Add the rye, vermouth, pineapple juice, and bitters to the mixing glass.

3. Using a bar spoon, stir for 30 seconds, or until chilled.

4. Discard the ice water, strain into the martini glass, and serve immediately.

CLOVE BITTERS

MAKES 6¼ OUNCES

Clove, a tiny, twig-shaped spice, smells like the holidays. But don't relegate it to just fall and winter cocktail duty. Its numbing menthol quality pairs well with mint and can take the heat out of a spicy drink. Use these bitters sparingly; a little goes a long way.

Create the tinctures required for this recipe using the procedure outlined in chapter 2 (see sidebar, "Your Tincture Primer," page 44).

PREP TIME: 1 MINUTE   INFUSING TIME: 29 DAYS

1½ ounces clove tincture
1 ounce orange tincture
1 ounce mint tincture

½ ounce cinchona bark tincture
2 ounces water
¼ ounce Rich Syrup (page 51)

1. In a clean bowl, combine the clove, orange, mint, and cinchona bark tinctures and mix thoroughly.

2. Add the water and syrup and, using a funnel, transfer to dark-colored bottles.

    TIP: Give each clove a whack with the side of a chef's knife to jump-start the infusion process.

DEADLY SIN

What better way to begin fall than with a little bourbon and sweet vermouth? They'll always be a classic combination, and with good reason. A hint of cherry flavor from the maraschino liqueur serves as a reminder of summer's last few days, and the clove bitters leave warming vanilla notes on the palate.

PREP TIME: 5 MINUTES

2 ounces bourbon
1 ounce sweet vermouth
¼ ounce maraschino liqueur

3 dashes Orange Bitters (page 50), or Regan's Orange Bitters No. 6
2 dashes Clove Bitters (page 159)
1 strip lemon zest, for garnish

1. Fill a mixing glass two-thirds full with ice, and fill a martini glass with ice water.

2. Add the bourbon, vermouth, maraschino liqueur, orange bitters, and clove bitters to the mixing glass.

3. Using a bar spoon, stir for 30 seconds, or until chilled.

4. Discard the ice water, strain into the martini glass, and garnish with the lemon zest.

SCOFFLAW

MAKES 1 DRINK

Scofflaw was a term coined during Prohibition to describe consumers of bootleg booze. Though it was originally intended as a pejorative, the word actually acquired a certain cachet after someone at Harry's New York Bar in Paris came up with a cocktail named after it. There's one reason it's survived to this day: It tastes absolutely brilliant.

PREP TIME: 5 MINUTES

1½ ounces rye whiskey
¾ ounce dry vermouth
1 ounce freshly squeezed
   lemon juice

½ ounce grenadine
3 dashes Orange Bitters (page 50),
   or Regan's Orange Bitters No. 6
2 dashes Clove Bitters (page 159)

1. Fill a shaker two-thirds full with ice, and fill a rocks glass with ice water.

2. Add the rye, vermouth, lemon juice, grenadine, orange bitters, and clove bitters to the shaker.

3. Shake for 10 to 15 seconds, or until chilled.

4. Discard the ice water, strain into the rocks glass, and serve immediately.

TIP: Filling serving glasses with ice water is a great way to chill them quickly, but if you plan on making a lot of cocktails for a party, you can skip this step by placing them in the refrigerator in advance.

CINNAMON BITTERS

MAKES 6¼ OUNCES

Cinnamon is a key spice for many of fall's beloved desserts. Whether you're making an apple cobbler, a pear crumble, or a pumpkin pie, classic American desserts just wouldn't be the same without it.

Cinnamon is also a nice addition to cocktails. Spirit-forward drinks based on bourbon, brandy, or rye can benefit from a few dashes of cinnamon bitters.

Create the tinctures required for this recipe using the procedure outlined in chapter 2 (see sidebar, "Your Tincture Primer," page 44).

PREP TIME: 1 MINUTE   INFUSING TIME: 29 DAYS

2 ounces cinnamon tincture
1½ ounces orange tincture
½ ounce cinchona bark tincture

2 ounces water
¼ ounce Rich Syrup (page 51)

1. In a clean bowl, combine the cinnamon, orange, and cinchona bark tinctures and mix thoroughly.

2. Add the water and syrup and, using a funnel, transfer to dark-colored bottles.

    TIP: For a milder cinnamon flavor, look for Ceylon cinnamon in spice shops.

WARD EIGHT

The Ward Eight cocktail was born at the Locke-Ober Café in Boston in 1898. It was named for Martin M. Lomasney's district, where he served as the infamous Democratic party overseer. Common lore has it that it was meant as a drink to commemorate his triumph in that year's campaign, but it was actually being served before the votes were completely counted. Talk about rocking the vote!

PREP TIME: 5 MINUTES

1½ ounces rye whiskey
1½ ounces freshly squeezed
    orange juice
½ ounce freshly squeezed
    lemon juice

¼ ounce grenadine
3 dashes Cinnamon Bitters
    (page 162)
1 strip lemon zest, for garnish

1. Fill a shaker two-thirds full with ice, and fill a rocks glass with ice water.

2. Add the rye, orange juice, lemon juice, grenadine, and bitters to the shaker.

3. Shake for 10 to 15 seconds, or until chilled.

4. Discard the ice water, strain into the rocks glass, and serve garnished with the lemon zest.

MANHATTAN IN THE FALL

MAKES 1 DRINK

Cinnamon bitters bring an elegant touch of fall to the classic drink. The Manhattan is an important cocktail because, according to Gary Regan, author of *The Joy of Mixology*, it is "the first drink that called for vermouth as a modifier," leading to the creation of an entire class of drinks. Its evolution gave rise to the Martinez, and subsequently the martini.

PREP TIME: 5 MINUTES

2 ounces bourbon

1 ounce sweet vermouth

3 dashes Cinnamon Bitters (page 162)

1 dash Angostura bitters

1 cinnamon stick, for garnish

1. Fill a mixing glass two-thirds full with ice, and fill a martini glass with ice water.

2. Add the bourbon, vermouth, cinnamon bitters, and Angostura bitters to the mixing glass.

3. Using a bar spoon, stir for 30 seconds, or until chilled.

4. Discard the ice water, strain into the martini glass, and garnish with the cinnamon stick.

TIP: Giving the cinnamon stick a firm whack with the side of your chef's knife will help release its flavor and aroma.

APPLE BITTERS

MAKES 6¼ OUNCES

Apple and spice, together they're oh so very nice. Apple bitters are a great addition to bourbon- and whiskey-based cocktails. They also play well with cocktails that have a hint of acidity.

Create the tinctures required for this recipe using the procedure outlined in chapter 2 (see sidebar, "Your Tincture Primer," page 44).

PREP TIME: 1 MINUTE   INFUSING TIME: 29 DAYS

1½ ounces apple tincture
½ ounce lemon tincture
½ ounce ginger tincture
½ ounce cinnamon tincture

½ ounce clove tincture
½ ounce horehound tincture
2 cups water
¼ ounce Rich Syrup (page 51)

1. In a clean bowl, combine the apple, lemon, ginger, cinnamon, clove, and horehound tinctures, and mix thoroughly.

2. Add the water and syrup and, using a funnel, transfer to dark-colored bottles.

TIP: When making the apple tincture, use just the peel of the apple so the bitters don't end up too sweet. Save the flesh for another use.

UNDER THE APPLE TREE

MAKES 1 DRINK

Imagine being in an apple orchard, inhaling the scent of all the crisp fruit at its peak—that's what this cocktail tastes like. This is a refreshing fall sipper that would be fantastic as an aperitif. Or it could also pair beautifully with food without overpowering it—perhaps a roast pork loin or glazed pork chops.

PREP TIME: 5 MINUTES

1½ ounces apple cider
1 ounce brandy
½ ounce Grand Marnier

½ ounce freshly squeezed lemon juice
3 dashes Apple Bitters (page 165)
1 strip lemon zest, for garnish

1. Fill a shaker two-thirds full with ice, and fill a martini glass with ice water.

2. Add the cider, brandy, Grand Marnier, lemon juice, and bitters to the shaker.

3. Shake for 10 to 15 seconds, or until chilled.

4. Discard the ice water, strain into the martini glass, and serve garnished with the lemon zest.

TIP: Different brands of apple cider vary in their sweetness; feel free to adjust the amount of lemon juice to suit your taste.

FALL FASHIONED

Once you've mastered the classic Old Fashioned cocktail, it's easy to put your own spin on it. Here's a fall variation that makes use of apple and clove bitters. This recipe calls for rye, but bourbon also works nicely.

PREP TIME: 5 MINUTES

1 sugar cube
3 dashes Apple Bitters (page 165)
3 dashes Clove Bitters (page 159)

2 ounces rye whiskey
1 strip lemon zest, for garnish

1. Place the sugar cube in a rocks glass and soak with the apple and clove bitters.

2. Using the flat end of a muddler, mash the ingredients until the sugar dissolves completely.

3. Fill the glass half full with ice, and then add the rye.

4. Stir for 30 seconds, or until well chilled, and serve garnished with the lemon zest.

Take It to the Next Level

Fall is a time to turn to the spice rack for inspiration. You've already gotten a sense of how different fall ingredients interact with different spirits, so now it's time to put some of that knowledge to use by creating your own fall bitters. A good place to start is thinking about some of your favorite things to make during this time of year—apple cider, pumpkin cheesecake, or roast pork with juniper, perhaps. To help you get started brainstorming, here are some more tips and ideas for bitters, cocktails, and pairings.

STOCK UP THE SPICE RACK. Here are traditional warm fall spices for you to try with some suggested cocktail pairings.

- CARAWAY SEEDS. Caraway seeds have a citrusy aroma and a slightly tart, savory flavor. You've probably seen them on a loaf of rye bread. They're great with gin-based cocktails.

- FENNEL SEEDS. Similar in appearance to caraway seeds, fennel has a licorice flavor when raw but turns savory when toasted. Pair with an anise liqueur, such as Fernet-Branca, or a citrusy cocktail.

- JUNIPER BERRIES. Juniper is the main flavoring component in London dry gins. This botanical has a flavor and aroma that's often compared to pine trees. Use with cocktails based on neutral white spirits or gin.

- NUTMEG. If the last time you had creamed spinach was memorable, it was probably thanks to this spice. Always buy nutmeg whole; ground nutmeg loses flavor and aroma quickly. It has a spicy, sweet, somewhat medicinal aroma. Use in cocktails based on amber spirits.

- **PEPPERCORNS.** Pink, green, black, and white—why not try them all? Each has a distinctive flavor that will give your cocktails an interesting twist.

- **STAR ANISE.** If cinnamon had a savory, meaty edge to it, this is what it would smell and taste like. Individual pods join at the center to form an exotic star shape. This would be fantastic in cocktails with foamy egg whites.

BITTERING AGENTS. Cinchona bark is a good match for the warmth of such spices as nutmeg, peppercorns, or star anise. Orris root's floral notes allow the flavor of caraway seeds, fennel seeds, or juniper berries to shine.

TIME TO PLAY. By now you know the drill. Here is a list of fall cocktails you may want to try, along with their key components and suggested bitters.

- **CLOVER CLUB.** Gin, lemon juice, egg white, grenadine, star anise bitters.

- **JACK ROSÉ.** Applejack, lemon juice, grenadine, green peppercorn bitters.

- **JERSEY COCKTAIL.** Applejack, hard cider, simple syrup, nutmeg bitters.

- **JOCKEY CLUB COCKTAIL.** Gin, amaretto, lemon juice, caraway seed bitters.

- **SATAN'S WHISKERS.** Gin, sweet and dry vermouth, orange juice, Grand Marnier, fennel bitters.

COMMERCIAL BITTERS

ANGOSTURA. An essential ingredient in many classic cocktails, including the Manhattan and Old Fashioned, this has strong notes of cardamom. These bitters are produced in Trinidad.

BAR KEEP ORGANIC LAVENDER BITTERS. This company, based in Monrovia, California, took home top honors at the 2009 Tales of the Cocktail event in New Orleans. This bitters recipe was one of the award-winning products.

THE BITTER END MOROCCAN BITTERS. Give your cocktails an exotic twist with this Moroccan-inspired bitters blend, made with coriander, lemon, mint, and cinnamon. The Bitter End is based in Santa Fe, New Mexico.

BITTERMENS GRAPEFRUIT HOPPED. Yet another popular offering from Bittermens, these bitters are an interesting blend of Pacific Northwest hops and grapefruit peel, suited to enhance cocktails based on light rum, tequila, or mezcal.

BITTERMENS XOCOLATL MOLE BITTERS. This bitters formula, an addictive combination of chocolate, cinnamon, and spices, put Bittermens on the map. Bittermens is now based in Brooklyn, New York.

DUTCH'S SPIRITS COLONIAL COCKTAIL BITTERS. This well-rounded product was inspired by ingredients from around the world, including Hungarian angelica, Pakistani red rose petals, French lavender, Egyptian chamomile, and Ceylon cinnamon.

FEE BROTHERS ORANGE BITTERS. Before Regan's came along, this was the only orange bitters in production in the United States, and it was practically impossible to find. The tides have turned with Fee Brothers, though, and the company offers a variety of flavors. But its orange bitters remain iconic.

PEYCHAUD'S. Created by Dr. Antoine Peychaud, these bitters—heavy on licorice and orange flavors—are an essential ingredient in classic cocktails, including the Sazerac.

REGAN'S ORANGE BITTERS NO. 6. Developed by Gary Regan, professional bartender and author of *The Joy of Mixology*, these bitters have a strong flavor of cardamom and dried orange peel.

SCRAPPY'S BITTERS. Don't let its seemingly simple offerings fool you. All of its products—from celery to Seville orange—are made with the finest organic ingredients.

GLOSSARY

ABSINTHE: A green anise-flavored spirit made with wormwood.

AGAVE NECTAR: Sap from the blue agave plant that is processed into a sweetener.

ARMAGNAC: A type of aged brandy made in the Gascony region in France.

AROMATIC BITTERS: Alcohol-based seasonings flavored with fresh or dried plant-based ingredients. They have an alcohol content of about 45 percent by volume.

BÉNÉDICTINE: A French brandy-based liqueur made with a proprietary blend of 27 botanicals, created by monks.

BRANDY: A spirit made from fermented mashed fruit.

CAMPARI: A dark red potable bitters with notes of citrus.

COGNAC: A type of aged brandy that comes from the area surrounding a town of the same name in France.

DRY VERMOUTH: A fortified wine flavored with botanicals, pale white in color. Usually mixed with clear spirits such as gin and vodka.

GOLDEN RUM: Rum that is aged in wooden barrels.

GRAND MARNIER: A brand of Cognac flavored with orange.

HERBSAINT: An anise-flavored absinthe substitute.

LIGHT RUM: Rum that is clear in color, aged briefly and filtered.

LIMONCELLO: A lemon-flavored liqueur from Italy.

LIQUEUR: A sweetened spirit flavored with botanicals, cream, or fruit.

MARASCHINO LIQUEUR: A sweet liqueur flavored with maraschino cherries. Luxardo is a popular brand.

MEZCAL: A spirit made from the agave plant. It is similar to tequila but usually has a smoky flavor.

MOONSHINE: An unaged white whiskey usually made in Tennessee or North Carolina.

POTABLE BITTERS: Liqueurs that have been sweetened and are flavored with botanicals. They generally have a low alcohol content and are drinkable. Examples include Jägermeister, Campari, and Fernet-Branca.

SWEET VERMOUTH: A fortified wine made with botanicals, pale red in color. Usually mixed with such spirits as bourbon, Scotch, or rye whiskey.

TRIPLE SEC: An orange-flavored liqueur essential for margaritas and similar drinks. Cointreau is a well-regarded brand of triple sec.

REFERENCES

Arnold, Eric. "Bitters and Seltzer: A Hangover Remedy That Actually Works." *The Booze Blog. Forbes.* March 15, 2010. www.forbes.com /sites/booze/2010/03/15/bitters-and-seltzer-a-hangover-remedy -that-actually-works/.

McLagan, Jennifer. *Bitter: A Taste of the World's Most Dangerous Flavor, with Recipes.* Berkeley: Ten Speed Press, 2014.

Meier, Frank. *The Artistry of Mixing Drinks.* France: Fryam Press, 1934. Reprint.

Parsons, Brad Thomas. *Bitters: A Spirited History of a Classic Cure-All with Cocktails, Recipes and Formulas.* Berkeley: Ten Speed Press, 2011.

Regan, Gary. *The Joy of Mixology.* New York: Clarkson Potter, 2003.

RESOURCES

SPIRITS

- 44° NORTH VODKA. www.44northvodka.com
- BEAM SUNTORY. www.beamsuntory.com
- BOMBAY SAPPHIRE. www.bombaysapphire.com
- BRUGAL RUM. www.brugal-rum.com
- BULLEIT. www.bulleit.com
- CALEDONIA SPIRITS. www.caledoniaspirits.com
- CAMPARI. www.campari.com
- COINTREAU. www.cointreau.com
- DEL MAGUEY. www.delmaguey.com
- DOLIN. www.dolin.fr
- DUTCH'S SPIRITS. www.dutchsspirits.com
- THE FAMOUS GROUSE. www.thefamousgrouse.com
- FRATELLI BRANCA. www.branca.it
- GRAND MARNIER. www.grand-marnier.com
- HANGAR 1 VODKA. www.hangarone.com
- JIM BEAM. www.jimbeam.com
- LIMONCELLO DI CAPRI. www.limoncello.com
- LUXCO. www.luxco.com

- SANDEMAN. www.sandeman.com

- SAZERAC. www.sazerac.com

- SOMBRA MEZCAL. www.sombramezcal.com

- SPRING 44. www.spring44.com

- TEQUILA AVIÓN. www.tequilaavion.com

- TEQUILA PATRÓN. www.patrontequila.com

- TRES AGAVES. www.tresagaves.com

COCKTAIL AND BITTERS RESOURCES

- DR. COCKTAIL. www.drcocktail.com

- DRINKBOY. www.drinkboy.com

- IMBIBE MAGAZINE. www.imbibemagazine.com

- JEFFREY MORGENTHALER. www.jeffreymorgenthaler.com

STORES

- BEVMO. www.bevmo.com

- BJ'S WHOLESALE CLUB. www.bjs.com

- COCKTAIL KINGDOM. www.cocktailkingdom.com

- COSTCO. www.costco.com

- DANDELION BOTANICAL COMPANY. www.dandelionbotanical.com

- KALUSTYAN'S. www.kalustyans.com

- PATEL BROTHERS. www.patelbros.com

- SAM'S CLUB. www.samsclub.com

- TENZING MOMO. www.tenzingmomo.com

RECIPE INDEX

INDEX

ABOUT THE AUTHOR

Will Budiaman is a New York City-based writer and recipe developer. He is a graduate of the International Culinary Center and is a recipe tester for the R&D kitchen at Maple, an app-based delivery service that brings seasonal dishes created by in-house chefs straight to people's doorsteps.

Previously, he served as a web producer for *Bon Appétit* and Epicurious, and as an editor at *The Daily Meal*, where he ran the test kitchen. He has ghost written three cookbooks. For more information or to purchase his other titles, visit willbudiaman.com.

CPSIA information can be obtained at www.ICGtesting.com
Printed in the USA
BVOW11s1221061115

425550BV00004B/4/P